Transgressive Corporeality

Transgressive Corporeality

The Body, Poststructuralism, and the Theological Imagination

Diane L. Prosser MacDonald

STATE UNIVERSITY OF NEW YORK PRESS

Published by
State University of New York Press, Albany

For information address State University of New York Press, State University Plaza, Albany, NY 12246

Production by Laura Starrett
Marketing by Terry Abad Swierzowski

Library of Congress Cataloging in Publication Date
MacDonald, Diane L. Prosser.
    Transgressive corporeality : the body, poststructuralism, and the theological imagination / Diane Louise Prosser.
        p.   cm.
    Includes bibliographical references and index.
    ISBN 0-7914-2487-1 : $57.50. — ISBN 0-7914-2488-X (pbk.) : $18.95
    1. Body, Human—Religious aspects—Christianity.   2. Sin.
3. Body, Human—Symbolic aspects.   I. Title.
BT741.2.P76   1995
233'.5—dc20   94-24727
                                                              CIP

10   9   8   7   6   5   4   3   2   1

Contents

For
Kathrina Louise Peckham Prosser
and Allen Mark Prosser

Acknowledgments

There have been many people in my life who through word and deed have shown me ways of living in "en-joy-ment" of this fragile, finite world. My parents, Kathrina Louise Peckham Prosser and Allen Mark Prosser have lived lives of strong faith and dedicated service to others. My siblings, Constance Ann Lawry, Carol Jean Smith, Janet Leigh Dorsey, Stephen Mark Prosser, and Susan Elizabeth Mahan are wise and wonderful in their own diverse pursuits and have been a source of encouragement to me. My children, Katya Louise MacDonald and Julian Peter MacDonald, have transgressed the order of my days in more ways than I could have imagined, but no less than I have come to appreciate, even delight in. And my friends, past and present, have through honesty, humor, and loving kindness provoked and enlivened my thinking and being.

Included among my friends, deserving special note, are those scholars who have shared their expertise with me during the conception and writing of this book. They include Carl A. Raschke, Jere Paul Surber, and James Kirk of the University of Denver; Delwin Brown, Dennis R. MacDonald, and Sheila Greeve Davaney of The Iliff School of Theology; and Lynn Ross-Bryant and Sam D. Gill of the University of Colorado at Boulder. I am grateful as well for the supportive and creative contexts of First Plymouth Congregational United Church of Christ in Englewood, Colorado, and The Iliff School of Theology in Denver, Colorado, and for the patience and encouragement of the editorial staff at the State University of New York Press.

To the extent that this work speaks with insight and hope about our current cultural situation, it is this collage of family, friends, and colleagues who are to be given thanks. And I do .

Preface

There are many ways to divide the world into binary categories. The infinite versus the finite, reason versus feeling, culture versus nature, soul versus body—these are some of the divisions that have given birth to the social structures and institutions of Western culture, as well as to the underlying patterns of thinking supporting them.

In recent years, while the specificity of these binary categories has changed, their underlying metaphysic has not. Even as we in the late-twentieth century have gravitated toward questions of race, class, gender, and sexual orientation, we have done so in large part through a call for change that bypasses those deep-seated sociohistorical constructs that keep the power dynamics of our lives the same. If those underlying constructs are embedded in the cultural imagination of our era, then real change can only be attained through a new imaginary, that is, a subversion of the imagineries forged out of binary modes of thinking and being, and the opening up of a space for something "other" to appear, something that speaks out of a radically different kind of subjectivity and relational ontology.

This study cannot bring a new imaginary into existence. Not only is that goal a false pretension of any theorizing effort, it is particularly illusory in respect to the kind of imaginary alluded to in poststructuralist discourse. For if this rather illusive, stylistically diverse, often inaccessible and usually irritating discourse of poststructuralism has anything constant running through it, it is the tacit understanding that the very enterprise of systematizing the complex phenomena of this world is a violent act, and that includes the enterprise of constructing a new cultural or, more specifically, religious imaginary.

So what is a theologian to do in order to contribute to the creation of a new imagination that resists the destructive power dynamics of binary modes of thinking and being? I suppose there are many interesting options. The one I've taken in this study is one of deconstruction and exploration— deconstruction of modes of binary thinking and being that have been dominate in post-Enlightenment Western culture, and exploration of the "remainders" of those systems as resources for a new style of being, subject to the critical assessment and practical wisdom of local practitioners.

In chapter 1, I set forth in more detail the tack of this endeavor, situating this trajectory of thought in the wake of Umberto Eco's intriguing portrayal of medieval body relations, Friedrich Nietzsche's critique of metaphysics as hatred for the body, and contemporary poststructuralist theologians' demonstration of the relation of modernist attitudes toward the body with modes of binary thinking. The style of writing in this chapter, while potentially annoying to some readers, is congruent with the goal of this project—that of transgressing the boundaries of our lives and thought in order to alter them. One cannot subvert conventional categories of thought by writing in a conventional style.

Chapters 2, 3, and 4 are focused respectively on the exploration of embodied existence by Maurice Merleau-Ponty, Michael Foucault, and Julia Kristeva. These theorists are three distinct voices, important to this project for providing examples of binarism within the cultural codes of post-Enlightenment society, revealing the dangers of such codes, and initiating an exploration of the "remainders" of these warring factions for alternative modes of subjectivity and relatedness. Although each chapter builds upon the one preceeding it, each can be read as a separate unit.

Chapter 5 begins with a summary of the major contributions of this trajectory of thinkers for the project of "transgressive corporeality," and then proceeds to apply these insights to questions of methodology in contemporary theology. The focus of this chapter is on the threshold of language and culture fed by elemental desires that lies between the realm of the "real" and that of the "symbolic." The imaginary of theology is fueled by the dominant images and/or metaphors of distinct religious traditions. And it is the play of these images that are shaped by and in turn give shape to the self-understandings and ethical practices of people in any particular setting. This chapter trys to give expression to a dynamic or "play" of imagery that escapes the "nay-saying" and "yea-saying" modes of theological construction. To "speak" this dynamic is to enter into a catharsis of the limits.

In summary, the goal of this book is not a new way of systematizing the movement of the sacred among us, but rather a transgression of those orders of thought and being that effectively resist the call of the sacred. To whatever degree I am successful in prompting such transgression for the reader, I consider this work worthwhile. For the true "bodies of transgression" are not those encapsulated in the words of a text, but those that move through the crossroads of everyday life with enlivening bursts of "wild love." It is my hope that this work will make us more discerning of that which prevents such outbursts and more daring in entering into the "blessed madness" of the limits.

CHAPTER ONE

Toward a Body of Un-Author-ized Transgression

Behold thou art fair, my beloved, behold thou art fair; thine eyes are as
doves (I said), and let me see thy face,
let me hear thy voice, for thy voice is
harmonious and thy face enchanting,
thou hast ravished my heart, my sister, thou hast ravished my heart with
one of thine eyes, with one chain of
thy neck, thy lips drop as the honey-
comb, honey and milk are under thy
tongue, . . . Who was she, who was
she who rose like the dawn, fair as
the moon, clear as the sun, terrible as
an army with banners?

—Umberto Eco,
The Name of the Rose

Transgressive Bodies According to Umberto Eco and Friedrich Nietzsche

In the middle of Umberto Eco's mystery of medieval monks and murders, in the dark underbelly of a grand monastic library, a young Benedictine monk, Adso of Melk, comes face to face with a marvelous and terrifying body.[1] It was the body of a peasant girl, a girl foreign to the order and language of monastic life, living outside its walls in the shadow of the towering Aedificium, and entering the sacred precincts only under cover of darkness and for the sole purpose of exchange.

She was a poor girl, unable to stave off her hunger and that of her family without using her body as a commodity, an exchange of flesh for flesh—her own for that of an ox. On some nights, she would carry off an ox heart, on others just bits of lung, but on all nights it was the same sweaty hands and fat, flush lips that grasped her body and flailed about the floor of the kitchen until satiated and exhausted. So it was with an expression of surprise, even wonder, that she beheld the young, shy Adso one night as he stood at the threshold of the kitchen. And carelessly, without thought of reward, she touched his cheek with the tips of her fingers and drew him near.

For Adso, such love was a deeply transgressive act. It was not simply a matter of disobedience. There were others who regularly transgressed the lofty codes of fourteenth-century Benedictine virtue by cavorting with flesh—sometimes even in the shadows of the abbey and often with a wink of approval from unexpected sources. Even the old, grave Jorge, guarantor of monastic authority and morality, knew the value of these transgressors. "Their presence is precious to us," he confesses, "it is inscribed in the plan of God, because their sin prompts our virtue, their cursing encourages our hymn of praise, their undisciplined penance regulates our taste for sacrifice, their impiety makes our piety shine."[2]

The transgression of the unregenerate, operating within an economy of exchange, an economy that thrived in darkness and in silence—this was an "authorized transgression."[3] Lacking the careless sensuality of innocence, this transgression set nothing ablaze—neither the passions of the inarticulate girl nor the ediface of monastic virtue erected on blood-soaked soil. Jorge had nothing to fear from such transgression. Indeed, it was "inscribed in the plan of God."

But Adso's transgression was a different matter altogether. Here was an innocent youth, uninitiated to the seductions of the flesh, a sensitive being, genuinely devoted to service of the holy. It was troubling enough for such a one to cross the threshold of saint and sinner, indulging in the base passions of the latter. This in itself had the potential to threaten the medieval "sorting myth" of god-fearers and pagans, of good and evil.

Yet even this spontaneous act of innocent passion was not in itself fully subversive. That which propelled Adso's transgression from that of potential danger to that of consuming conflagation was the intertwining of such innocent sensuality with the language of Scripture. The real transgression, that which threw the young monk into the turbid waters of confusion and ultimately shook the foundations of Jorge's world, was the transgression of language. In the ecstasy of the moment, driven by a desire beyond his control and confronted with a body and complex of sensations for which he had no name, Adso resorted to the use of sacred words for expressing the delirium of the body.

> What did I feel? What did I see? I remember only that the emotions of the first moment were bereft of any expression, because my tongue and my mind had not been instructed in how to name sensations of that sort. Until I recalled other inner words, heard in another time and in other places, spoken certainly for other ends, but which seemed wondrously in keeping with my joy in that moment, as if they had been consubstantially to express it. Words pressed into the caverns of my memory rose to the (dumb) surface of my lips, and I forgot that they had served in Scripture or in the pages of the saints to express quite different, more radiant realities. *But was there truly a difference between the delights of which the saints had spoken and those that my agitated spirit was feeling at that moment?* At that moment the watchful sense of difference was annihilated in me. And this, it seems to me, is precisely the sign of rapture in the abysses of identity.[4]

By doing this, by confusing the language of love for God with love for an illicit, earthly body, Adso set into play a host of questions culminating in a suspicion of the capability of language to discriminate between the realms of truth and falsehood and thereby represent an independent, transcendent, stable order of truth. Language was fluid. Some words evoked multiple meanings; a single meaning could be evoked by multiple words. There was no direct correspondence between language and reality and therefore no firm terrain of signification upon which to build one's edifice of truth, religious or otherwise.[5]

Although Adso himself struggled valiently to regain firm terrain, his teacher, the unruly and brilliant Franciscan, William of Baskerville, understood the depth of the dilemma and accepted its consequences. Toward the end of the story, when William realized that his quest for an overarching plan for the abbey's murders was futile, he admitted that there was no plot—either for the events in the abbey or for the universe as a whole. "I behaved stubbornly," he confesses, "pursuing a semblance of order, when I should have known well that there is no order in the universe."[6] His imagined plan had only accidentally helped to solve the murders. In a language not fully medieval, William reflects on truth as a ladder "built to attain something." Once used, it should be thrown away.[7]

For William, the most pressing problem of the abbey was not the threat of destabilizing events upon the structures of metaphysical truth. For him, in contrast to Jorge as well as the young Adso, the dilemma shifted from that of unruly bodies to that of unitary, fixed truths. The real problem, he concludes, is the arrogance of those who claim to hold the truth, the grimness of those whose certainty is never seized by doubt. "Perhaps the mission of those who love mankind," he says, "is to make people laugh at the truth, to make truth laugh, because the only truth lies in learning to free ourselves from insane passion for the truth."[8] For William then, the unruly, indescribable body is important as that which resists the mechanisms of repressive truths. As the "remainder" of all forms of representation, it eludes the grasp of domination and points toward another way.[9]

In this way, through the meanderings of monks and metaphor, Eco brings into the noonday light the difference between a sickly "authorized transgression" that is the soil for edifices of religiously sanctioned virtue, and the "unauthorized transgression" of an innocent sensuality imbued with spirit. From out of the belly of "authorized transgression," a transgression of exchange and exploitation, institutions and structures of morality are born. Put otherwise, the rape of the innocent is the silent substructure of institutions that set a rigid dividing line between good and evil and then enforce the good. It is all too often the womb of church, of mosque, and of synagogue, as well as that of the state.

But such structures in Eco's story were set ablaze. Through the heat of a tender passion, a spark was ignited that brought about the apocalypse.[10] And only in its aftermath, in the scattered ruins of charred walls capped by the open beams of a roof now collapsed—only in the aftermath of such massive destruction did the remain(s) appear: some birds, a snake, ivy, and a few fragments of parchment. These fragments, gathered together by the elderly Adso, contained no unified message and yet constituted an "oracle" that spoke through his writing, an oracle of a god that "*ist ein lauter Nichts, ihn rührt kein Nun noch Hier.*"[11]

Such is the transgressive body and sensuous remainder of a medieval rationality as imagined by a linguist of the South. But for such a body to emerge in recent days in the more northern and ethereal realms of philosophy and theology, a barbarian would be needed—one who roamed the wild spaces outside towns, dwelt in a cave, communed with a bird and a snake, and danced to the rhythms of a god adorned with ivy.[12] This old barbarian, of course, is none other than Friedrich Nietzsche's Zarathustra. Indeed, the cry that echoes throughout Nietzsche's writing, shattering the dominant religious and political "truth" structures of his day and writhing toward the articulation of an alternative "ontology of relationship" is precisely the cry of the body. By listening to this cry, this barbaric voice of "wild wisdom,"[13] we will hear more clearly the challenges of a transgressive corporeality as it pertained to the problematic of philosophy in the latter half of the nineteenth century.

To bring such challenges into our era, especially in the wake of the ravages of the twentieth century and its growing powers of destruction, the cries of new barbarians or speakers of "wild wisdom" must be heard. Such poststructuralist "wild" ones, like Nietzsche before them, are characterized by two impulses held in critical tension, that is, the shattering of edifices of truth girded in relations of exchange along with a persistent retrieval and exploration of truth's remain(s). For some, like Nietzsche's "last man," such remain(s) as love, creation, and longing have been forgotten.[14] For the "wild ones," these and other remain(s) are not only remembered, but retrieved as fuel for a new thinking, an igniting of the theological imagination in an age grown weary by cynicism and despair.

For the remainder of this chapter, in an attempt to clarify the problematic of a transgressive corporeality, we will first turn to Nietzsche for a depiction of those "despisers of the body" who esteem "sickly, ugly bodies," over against those who love "healthy, natural bodies." Following this, we will turn to the writings of two contemporary radical theologians in order to augment Nietzsche's "body" thinking by ciphoning it through the events of the twentieth century and bringing it into the specificity of the theological discourse. This chapter will conclude with a preliminary theoretical framework for use in subsequent chapters in our exploration of the body philosophies of three French writers: Maurice Merleau-Ponty, Michel Foucault, and Julia Kristeva.

In turning to Nietzsche, it comes as no surprise that the primary target of his philosophical hammer was that cluster of grim authorities, religious and philosophical, who were best characterized as "despisers of the body."[15] From Socrates at the "daylight of reason"[16] to Immanuel Kant, to nineteenth-century German Lutherans, the "healthy body" was hated, castrated,[17] regulated, tamed,[18] annihilated,[19] idealized, sentimentalized, systematized, tranquilized, and desensualized.[20]

And how was this massive denial accomplished across such a vast span of time and space? In every case, the motivating impulse was a "will-to-truth," a will to that which is constant and unitary, a will that tended to spin out in a variety of "conceptual cobwebs" but which was always inscribed in the culture in its structures of morality.[21] For Nietzsche, the deepest challenge of his day, as it had been for a long time, was the problem of violations of the body that were implicit in and complicit with any philosophical or theological attempt to reduce the irreducible phenomena of the temporal world into a single, fixed truth by dividing all that is into the oppositional categories of good and evil. It was bad enough that such truths had thrived from the days of classical Greece to the present and from the far away shores of the Indian Sea to those of the Mediterranean.[22] It was even worse that such truths posed as the best of humankind, as the cultural apex of the accomplishments of great thinkers and esteemed artists. It was the worst of injuries that such truths were girded in hidden foundations of denial and abuse.

Nietzsche's outrageous response, while not defensible in every respect, particularly in light of the events of the twentieth century, was yet, in its keenness of perception and intensity of passion, a somewhat fitting response. How could he have been rational when rationality was defined by the truthful? How could he have been moral when morality itself was the problem? Although there is never only one way to confront such entrenched monstrosities as culturally sanctioned "go(o)ds," the only salvific way is that of wholehearted subversion. And to that end, Nietzsche threw all that he had: heart, will, and mind.

One can read Nietzsche's strategy of response as doubled. On the one hand, the pathos that drew most of his energy was the rage, the impulse to philosophize with a hammer, disempowering the architectonic of unitary truths by revealing their innermost secrets. Thus, armed with the potent weapon of laughter, he lashed out at the heart of his society's social conventions and structures. Christianity, he called a "hangman's metaphysics,"[23] a "herd religion," and "the great unholy lie."[24] German art was "a holiday for the spirit, the wits, and the heart."[25] And perhaps most disturbing to those working in academic settings even in different times and places, education was for him "the model of sublime monotony in action."[26]

All of the above, along with several other structures of high culture, were, according to Nietzsche, rooted in the "anti-aesthetic," that is, "the desire to make [everything] comprehensible; the desire to make [it] practical, useful, exploitable"[27]—in other words, hatred for the body. Even in laughter, Nietzsche was a raging beast, exposing the utilitarian base of such truths and struggling toward an alternative response.

But if one hears only the rage, feeling only the bite of Nietzsche's cold, wintry winds, then one has not fully encountered this amazing and troubling prophet. For as he says of all those "smoky, room-temperature, used-up, wilted, fretful souls" who surround him, "they hear only my winter winds whistling—and not that I also cross warm seas, like longing, heavy, south winds."[28] Nietzsche's "south winds," like those blowing through *The Name of the Rose* in the intertwining of two young lovers, are the winds of a sensuality emanating from the "higher, healthy body."

And here, at a critical juncture, in the articulation of this "higher body," Nietzsche enters rough terrain, a move for which he can be commended, and yet terrain within which he stumbles and strays. The higher body, associated by Nietzsche with a mode of existence exemplified by the ancient Greeks, and especially with a Dionysiac mode of intoxication for life, is appealing in its fulness, its fierce courage, deep emotion, and spontaneity. This for his was the spur of creativity, the energy of the universe propelling itself into the cyclical and spiraling forms of eternal recurrence. As such, "the entire evolution of the spirit" becomes not a question of the human, but rather, "a question of the body."[29]

Such a body was enticing in Nietzsche's day and would continue to be so today were it not for its susceptibility to the very diseases that Nietzsche tried so desperately to overcome. In the ironies of history, the higher, healthy body in the first half of this century became a war cry of the Fascists. The Dionysiac delirium for religious ecstasy became in this case a delirium of love for family, nation, and race—one which needed to expel the impurities of the body politic in order to restore its health.[30] Today this body is given new life in the hedonistic subcultures of technological society—from the drug-induced frenzies and fantasies of satanic cult groups to the equally mind-blowing escapades of devotees of hard rock.[31] Given the incorporation of Nietzsche's higher body to these enterprises of hate and destruction, it would be dangerously naive to embrace this body too quickly and uncritically. More needs to be thought about this lure before we too enter its terrain and stumble.

Thus, our turn to the writing of today's proponents of "wild wisdom" is more than a simple updating of Nietzsche. Granted that this prophet was a voice in the wilderness of nineteenth-century philosophy, and granted that his cry echoes into our era in multiple ways—not only in the exploits of militarism and terrorism, but also, with a quite different ring, through the writing of those who rage against the truths of body despisers in contemporary form—nonetheless, a new barbarism must address the uncanny ability of structures of truth to commandeer and make their own their fiercest opposition. How does a voice such as Nietzsche's become assimilated to truths even uglier than those he himself had opposed? How does he become the hero of those who destroy the "body" in ever more terrifying ways?

It seems to me that the importance of this century's radical theologians, in wrestling with today's truths and their "remains(s)," is their responsiveness to Nietzsche's challenge along with the additional challenge of how that cry has gone astray and become itself part of the problem. Against all despisers of the body, we must give voice to the "sensuous remainder" or transgressive body that is, as Mark C. Taylor suggests, the "reveilation" of the holy.[32] We must unleash the powers of such a body in all its fright and beauty. And yet, what this means and how to do it without falling into the hands of today's body despisers is not yet clear.

Some twentieth-century poststructuralist theologians, however, are leading the way to a clearing. Mark C. Taylor and Sharon D. Welch are among those who, like Nietzsche before them and yet more radically than he, are exposing the faults of totalizing structures of truth and exploring their remain(s).[33] Although the range of their intellectual adventures is much wider and deeper than can be fathomed here, we will draw on those aspects of their thinking that help shape the problematic of transgressive corporeality and lead to a framework for an exploration of other philosophies of body.

To summarize our investigation so far, edifices of truth—depicted by Eco as the truth-structures of fourteenth-century Benedictine monasticism, and by Nietzsche as the fixed, unitary truths of Western philosophy and theology—are shaped by a binary logic of good and evil and operate out of hidden strategies of exploitation. Because these truth structures are totalizing endeavors, continually struggling to set perimeters for the irreducible elements of life, their greatest enemy is the body that eludes their control. For both Nietzsche and Eco, the body is both indescribable (unrepresentable) and sensuous. For both, it is a body of such power that it can ignite the spark that explodes into a raging and roaring fire, reducing a grand and mighty truth, including its almighty God, to a charred ruin. These ruins are not the end of truth but its brokenness—its openness to the sky and earth and to their material remain(s).

Corporeality as Critique in Poststructuralist Theology

Although Eco, as a twentieth-century linguist, understands the role of language in the dissolution and reconstruction of edifaces of truth, more needs to be said about this "linguistic turn" as it pertains to contemporary theology. In a book entitled *Deconstruction and Theology*, published in 1982, Carl A.

Raschke in the lead article begins his exploration of language with a cry from Nietzsche's madman in the town's marketplace.

"Whither is God?" he cried; "I will tell you. *We have killed him*—you and I. All of us are his murderers. But how did we do this? How could we drink up the sea? Who gave us the sponge to wipe away the entire horizon? What were we doing when we unchained this earth from its sun? Whither is it moving now? Whither are we moving? Away from all suns? Are we not plunging continually? Backward, sideward, forward, in all directions? Is there still any up or down? Are we not straying as through an infinite nothing? . . . Do we hear nothing as yet of the noise of the gravediggers who are burying God? Do we smell nothing as yet of the divine decomposition? Gods, too, decompose. God is dead. God remains dead. And we have killed him."[34]

Who, we still ask today, is this God? How did he die? And what is the "nothing" that remain(s) in the decomposition of the divine?

As Raschke argues in this article and elsewhere,[35] the God of classical realism who functioned as a lynchpin for correspondence theories of truth, securing the referential relation between concepts and objects, was replaced in the seventeenth century by the "idols" or constructions of the modern subject. This took many forms. It began with the Cartesian turn to consciousness as a new foundation for certainty, continued through the architectonic of Kant's universal conditions and structures of consciousness, and eventually led to a positing of the historical conditions of modern consciousness, that is, the grammar and structure of language.

Although the content of these constructs changed, shifting from Descartes' "ego" to Wittgenstein's "grammar," the underlying structure of reference remained the same. In Derrida's now well-known formulation, the logocentric structure of reference links a signifier to a signified through an Archimedean point of reference or "transcendental signified," that is itself outside the play of signification and yet secures the meaningfulness of the signifying process.[36] The idols themselves may change. The "transcendental signifieds" may emerge with different forms and faces. But as each new idol takes its place on the throne of the deposed God, it performs the same basic function as each of its predecessors, stabilizing the play of signification by attesting to the reliability of language, that is, its reference to a stable, ordered reality external to itself. In Nietzsche's terms, each new idol is but a different version of the old "will-to-truth."

In order to appreciate the importance of dethroning such pretenders to truth, more needs to be said about the relationship of these idols to historical structures of the modern era. In a move consonant with Nietzsche, but going beyond him in depth and breadth of analysis, Mark C. Taylor, in *Erring: a Postmodern A/theology* and subsequent writings,[37] exposes the relationship between linguistic structures of representation tied to "the actual or possible presence of a transcendental signified" and social, political, economic structures of domination.[38]

Both economies—that of representation and that of domination—operate within structures of reference that claim to refer to the "other" and yet, in actuality, are structures of self-reference which use the "other," whether human, divine, or otherwise, as fodder for the "becoming" of the sovereign subject. This philosophy of self-relation, initiated by Descartes, reaches its apex in the speculative idealism of Hegel. In Taylor's words: "The Hegelian Idea that grounds all reality is a structural totality in which everything becomes *itself* in and through *its own* other. Because otherness and difference are essential components of self-identity . . . relationship to otherness and difference is, in the final analysis, *self*-relationship."[39]

Thus, the "other" for the totalizing or sponge-like structures of modern philosophical projects is an "other" of utilitarian value in the constitution of the self. When the "other" resists this role, when it refuses to be used or consumed by means of the autotelic processes of the sovereign subject, its territory is then invaded and its otherness colonized.[40]

The economy of representation is an economy of domination based on the subject's use and abuse of everything "other" than itself within the self-constituting process. Therefore, the idols of the marketplace are not simply silly illusions as pretenders to truth, but dangerous fictions, posing as the best and highest of truths and yet in reality girded in the most despicable forms of utilitarian relations. Although the exposure of these idols as fictive frauds cannot lead to the establishment of new fixed, unitary truths, it can, by breaking the grip of hegemonies of truth operating within a cultural setting, create the conditions for the emergence of a revitalized and radicalized imagination and style of being. The real motivation for the dethroning of all idols of modernity is the subversion of economies of domination and the creation of conditions for the emergence of radically different possibilities of relatedness among all the inhabitants of the earth.

But how are these idols of the marketplace to be knocked off their thrones? And what does this have to do with the body? As set forth by Taylor in *Altarity*, that which has the potential to subvert the structures of representation/domination is neither outside of and thereby absent from these structures of self-relation nor enclosed within and thereby fully present to them. Rather, drawing upon a range of "limit" concepts from Kant to Hegel to Kierkegaard to Derrida, Taylor explores the limits of structures of representation as resources for the subversion of modernist idols and as spurs to new religious or "a/theological" thinking.

As an example of this exploration of liminal remainders, Taylor, in the last chapter of *Tears* entitled "How to Do Nothing With Words," brings into play the "nothing" that remains at the limits of economies of representation. In this "nothing," one recognizes the remain(s) of Nietzsche's decomposing God as well as those of the monastery's Aedificium gathered by the elderly Adso. By persisting in the writing of such remain(s), particularly in their exposure of the latent fascism of today's "theo-logy" and "theo-ry," Taylor helps rekindle an imagination responsive to the cry of the body.[41]

Still, despite the perceptiveness and intrigue of these explorations, there is one aspect of Taylor's "parapraxis" which calls for further thought.[42] In its depiction of the impact of "nothing" upon the structures of representation, Taylor's writing reverberates with the full force and feeling of Nietzsche's wintry winds. Such writing wounds, tears, rends, and then wounds, tears, and rends again—almost without remainder, certainly without relief. From where, we might ask, comes healing? Whence come fragments of hope? Perhaps the impact of Nietzsche's warm, heavy winds from more southern states has not yet reached these northern realms. Perhaps they are still on the way.[43]

If such southern winds are those that stirred Zarathustra's

desire to dance, even to dance with words, then these winds are not foreign to the imaginative realm of other postmodern writers, including the feminist theology of Sharon D. Welch. Although Welch, in *Communities of Solidarity and Resistance* and *A Feminist Ethic of Risk*[44] does not make a direct analogy between her "dance with life" and that of Nietzsche's dancing deity, her writing does resonate with the insights and passions of other writers of "wild wisdom." Like Taylor, she decries the utopian ideals or "truths" of theologies rooted in utilitarian relations, or, in her own terminology, in an "ethic of control."[45] Her own contribution to an analysis of the problematic of theology includes the exposure of an "erotics of domination" implicit in twentieth-century theology by virtue of its "valorization of absolute power."[46] According to Welch, through such seemingly rational and virtuous ideals as freedom and justice, new normative unities are envisioned and established in liberal ethical theory and theology.[47] These unities are in actuality part of the problem in that they have their own exclusionary devices and perpetuation of relations of domination, now made more dangerous by virtue of their mystification by the mask of virtue.[48]

In her exploration of the material conditions or remain(s) spawning an "emancipatory conversation," Welch suggests that this entails a turn to body,[49] that is, to "sensuous immersion in a world that outruns the subject."[50] The desire of this body threatens to subvert the totalizing forces of the "erotics of domination" through a "deeply abiding love"[51] of the finite world, one that brings a "resilient, fragile, healing power"[52] to those wounded and torn by present-day truths. In this insightful and moving exploration of suffering and love as expressed in the novels of African-American women, Welch links what we are calling "un-author-ized transgression" to an innocence intrinsic to the "resilient connections" of people in solidarity against particular, historical forms of injustice. Like Adso in Eco's novel and yet with the astuteness of a twentieth-century poststructuralist theologian, Welch also uses sacred words to express bodily connections. In her words, the "healing connections of grace" among those who with "sheer holy boldness" struggle to speak "the truth of their lives"—these connections *are* the divine.[53]

Following in the wake of these adventuresome thinkers of "sensuous remain(s)," we are now ready to give preliminary articulation to "transgressive corporeality" as it pertains to the discourse of contemporary theology. In the shaping of this alternative, we are reminded of important distinctions made by those in our lead. First, there was the distinction so brilliantly depicted in Eco's novel between the "authorized transgression" of oppressive religious structures rooted in relations of exchange and the "unauthorized transgression" of a sensuous intercourse expressed in the poetry of sacred language.

This led to a somewhat analogous division, scattered throughout Nietzsche's writings, between the "diseased body" of body despisers and idol-worshipers, and the "higher, healthy body" of devotees of a dancing deity. Such "wild wisdom" was continued in corrected form in the work of Taylor and Welch. With varied styles and agendas, these writers cite the difference between "logocentric theologies" girded in structures of oppressive relations and a/centric or a/theological thinking, which subverts these structures through a "writing" or poeisis of their limits. That these limits may include such diverse discursive territories as the "nothing" of deconstructive strategies perusing the "history of thought" and the "resilient connections" of communities of solidarity and resistance reflected upon in theologies of liberation, confirms the nature of such limits as nonunified, unrepresentable, and still calling for further thought.

For us, this call leads to the positing of another distinction, hopefully in line with those just cited. This is the difference between a corporeality or "corp-o-logy" of author-ized transgression and a corporeality or "corp-o-sant" of un-author-ized transgression. The former is indicative of all contemporary structures or "corporations" which create and then perpetuate mystifications of domination under the auspices of the idols of self-aggrandizing power or privilege. The logic of "corp-o-logy" is tied to the "transcendental signifieds" of consciousness (an ego-logical corp-o-logy); of unified, universal experience (an empir(e)-ical corp-o-logy); or of linguistic structures (a grammot-ical corp-o-logy). "Corp-o-logy" then is a positivism of the body that takes on different names and forms within rationalism, empiricism, romanticism, liberalism, and structuralism, but has the same "effects of truth," that is, the attempted closure and control of the irreducible, sensuous body.

Our alternative, the "corp-o-sant" body of "un-author-ized transgression," is a holy body associated with the brush discharge or flaming phenomenon sometimes seen in stormy weather on the upper masts of ships. Given St. Elmo's identity as the patron saint of sailors, this seemingly self-starting flame became known as St. Elmo's fire. A "corp-o-sant" then is a body sparked by the "nonoriginal origin" of atmospheric tensions and creating a flame which threatens the structure of the ship, exposing it to the abyss of the sea. This body, being part of a structure and yet outside the structure's control, is necessarily a body of limits. In terms of the division just noted, a "corp-o-sant" is a body of the limits of today's "corp-o-logies." It is a body at the limits of "economies of representation" and at the margins of "economies of domination."

This "corp-o-sant" body of nonoriginal or "un-author-ized" transgression is the site then for the crossing of the forces of sky and sea. Some forces that ravish the body of the ship are philosophical, generated by tensions between truth and error, reason and madness. Some are political, spawned in the inter-action of order and chaos, the powerful and the powerless. Still others are psychological, birthed through the intercourse of the conscious with the unconscious and of thinking with feeling. All these winds feed the gales that make the sails of the ship "rounded and taut and trembling,"[54] the gales of winds religious and moral—the clashing of God(s) and world, of good and evil.

And although there is no haven from such storms, no serene harbor of peace and calm, no cure for the suffering and struggles of life, there is a choice. One can take down the sails that catch these winds in a futile attempt to escape their effects, or instead, one can hoist the sails up to the heights, opening them to north and south winds alike, until they "tremble with the violence of the spirit(s)."[55]

This study is an attesting to and testing of some of the winds—philosophical, political, psychological and ultimately religious and moral—that have shaped and are shaping "bod-ies" in the course of post-Enlightenment Western culture. In the lead of those heading such winds in our century is Maurice Merleau-Ponty, a philosopher known for the identification and critique of "objective thought," that is, forms of empiricism and idealism that have tried to enclose and tame the body. The limit that resists such closure for Merleau-Ponty is an "aesthetics of body," first presented within the terminology of a phenomenology of perception, and then radicalized through a shift into the dynamics of flesh, the field of Being as language.

Michel Foucault will historicize and politicize our course by naming the shifting winds of "rationalities" as they have been inscribed within and upon the bodies of people in different historical periods and places. And while the winds tested by Foucault are by and large cold and savage, the site of their inscription is also the site of resistance. The body for Foucault is not only the material "representation of authority" in Western culture. It remain(s) as well the source for the emergence of new alternatives through an "aesthetics of existence."

What Foucault only hints at in his body of inscription and resistance, Kristeva explores further within the categories of psychoanalysis and linguistics. "La Mère qui jouit" as a body of "abjection" is neither enclosed within the control mechanisms of the "law of the Father" nor relegated to the primal, undifferentiated silence of the Freudian and Lacanian "unconscious." Even though Kristeva may not be fully consistent in her thinking of the body of the "mother's joy" as a limit, she does try to hold in critical tension the structures of authorized transgression with those unruly, resilient connections of ecstatic human relatedness which threaten such structures. Over against the (ex)tensions of modernist "corp-o-logies," she gives expression to a gendered "corp-o-sant" of (re)tension, a body reverberating with an "aesthetics of relatedness."[56]

With these philosophies of body taking the lead, our own adventure of "un-author-ized transgression" will move from phenomenology to poststructuralism, from the flesh of artistic vision to the flesh of penal colonies to the flesh of ec-static relations, and from a wide-ranging interdisciplinary conversation back to theology. In all of this meandering, we must beware of letting our eyes venture too far from the earthly things of sea and sky or of allowing our ears to venture beyond hearing range of Nietzsche's plaintive cry, a cry of return to the body.

> Remain faithful to the earth, my brothers, with the power of your virtue. Let your gift-giving love and your knowledge serve the meaning of the earth. This I beg and beseech you. Do not fly away from earthly things and beat with your wings against eternal walls. Alas, there has always been so much virtue that has flown

away. Lead back to the earth the virtue that flew away, as I do—back to the body, back to life, that it may give the earth a meaning, a human meaning.[57]

Notes

1. Umberto Eco, *The Name of the Rose*, trans. William Weaver (New York: Harcourt, Brace, Jovanovich, 1983), 246.

2. Ibid., 476.

3. Over against the tendency of some theorists to present "carnival" as socially and politically liberating, Eco insists that most forms of carnival, including sexual excesses, are regulated transgressions that ultimately "remind us of the existence of the rule." Not reversals, but violations from the threshold serve as truly transgressive acts. See Theresa Coletti, *Naming the Rose: Eco, Medieval Signs, and Modern Theory* (Ithaca, N.Y.: Cornell University Press, 1988), 139–41.

4. Eco, *The Name of the Rose*, 244–45. Emphasis mine.

5. For this insight regarding the play of language in Eco's novel, I am indebted to two sources: Carl A Raschke, "Fire and Roses: Toward Authentic Post-Modern Religious Thinking," *Journal of the American Academy of Religion* 58 (Winter 1990): 671–89, and Theresa Coletti, *Naming the Rose*. Note that the most despicable heretics from Jorge's perspective were those who condoned such confusions. St. Francis of Assisi, the founder of the order to which William of Baskerville belonged, was a principal offender.

6. Eco, *The Name of the Rose*, 492.

7. Ibid., 492. Note that this is a critique of truth as the adequation of word to object and not necessarily exclusive of other notions of truth, including the one being developed in this study.

8. Ibid., 491.

9. This notion of remainder or "reste" is explored by Mark C. Taylor in his presentation of Derrida's writings in *Altarity*

(Chicago: University of Chicago Press, 1987), 255–303. That this is, according to Taylor, a "sensuous remainder" (341) alluding to "transgression" and "remains of the sacred" (346) is a spur to my exploration of "transgressive corporeality."

10. I am not suggesting here either that this "illicit" encounter by itself set off the fire or that the fire was an unmitigated good. The sexual encounter was a catalyst for the fire because, like a book of laughter by Aristotle, it was one of those confusions of the boundaries that couldn't be tolerated by those ensnared in modes of binary thinking. In protecting his unadulterated truth from such confusions, Jorge caused the fire that ultimately destroyed the library. Here then is a prime example of the kind of destruction that is unleashed by the guardians of fixed, unitary, and pristine truths.

11. Eco, *The Name of the Rose*, 501.

12. Note that the remains of the monastic aedificium following the fire are the same as those associated with Zarathustra in Nietzsche's writings.

13. Friedrich Nietzsche, *Thus Spoke Zarathustra: A Book for All and None*, trans. Walter Kaufman (New York: Viking Penguin, 1966), 197.

14. Ibid., 17.

15. Nietzsche, *Thus Spoke Zarathustra*, 34–35.

16. Friedrich Nietzsche, *Twilight of the Idols/The Anti-Christ*, trans. R. J. Hollingdale (New York: Viking Penguin, 1968), 33.

17. Friedrich Nietzsche, *The Will to Power*, trans. Walter Kaufman and R. J. Hollingdale (New York: Vintage Books, 1967), 253, 207.

18. Nietzsche, *Twilight of the Idols*, 55.

19. Nietzsche, *Thus Spoke Zarathustra*, 112.

20. Nietzsche, *The Will to Power*, 141, 407, 131, 139, 434.

21. Ibid., 249 and 317, 145.

22. On pp. 175–79 of *Thus Spoke Zarathustra*, Nietzsche applauds the Laws of Menu for their "order of castes" reflecting

the "natural order," and denounces those "truth-sayers" (like Vedantic philosophers) who teach equality. Not only is Nietzsche here sadly misinformed about the damaging effects of these laws in Hindu life, but his war against the mediocrity of the herd here takes a turn for the worse rather than for the better. Unfortunately, this ugly elitism pervades Nietzsche's writing and tarnishes its otherwise beautiful wisdom.

23. Nietzsche, *Twilight of the Idols*, 53.

24. Nietzsche, *The Will to Power*, 127, 117.

25. Ibid., 84.

26. Ibid., 473.

27. Ibid., 359.

28. Nietzsche, *Thus Spoke Zarathustra*, 174.

29. Nietzsche, *The Will to Power*, 358.

30. The complex issue regarding Nietzsche's responsibility for the use of his writing to support the Fascist movement cannot be fully decided here. Yet, in my opinion, Nietzsche's concept of body is not healthy to the extent that it *too* rests on the utilitarian use of the other for the achievement of its heights.

31. For a depiction of the link between Nietzsche and these groups, see Carl A. Raschke, *Painted Black: From Drug Killings to Heavy Metal—the Alarming True Story of How Satanism Is Terrorizing Our Communities* (New York: Harper and Row, 1990).

32. Taylor, *Altarity*, 41–47 and 340–53.

33. There are of course others who fit this category, including Charles E. Winquist, author of *Epiphanies of Darkness: Deconstruction in Theology* (Philadelphia: Fortress Press, 1986), a work especially pertinent to "body" as it pertains to the "limits" of psychoanalysis and theology.

34. Carl A. Reschke, "The Deconstruction of God" in *Deconstruction and Theology*, eds. Thomas J. J. Altizer and others (New York: Crossroad Pub. Co., 1982), 1–2, quoting from Friedrich Nietzsche, *The Gay Science*, trans. W. Kaufman (New York: Random House, 1974), 181.

35. Two of Raschke's works especially pertinent to this study are *The Alchemy of the Word: Language and the End of Theology* (Missoula, Montana: Scholars Press, 1979), and *Theological Thinking: An In-quiry* (Atlanta: Scholars Press, 1988.)

36. Raschke, "The Deconstruction of God," 7–11.

37. Aside from *Altarity* already noted, see Mark C. Taylor, *De-constructing Theology* (New York: The Crossroad Publishing Co., 1982); *Erring: A Postmodern A/theology* (Chicago: University of Chicago Press, 1984); *Tears* (Albany: State University of New York Press, 1990); *Disfiguring* (Chicago: University of Chicago Press, 1992) and *Nots* (Chicago: University of Chicago Press, 1993).

38. Taylor, *Tears*, 206.

39. Ibid., 93.

40. Taylor, *Erring*, 29.

41. See Mark C. Taylor, "The Politics of Theo-ry," 59 *Journal of the American Academy of Religion* (Spring 1991), 1–37.

42. "Parapraxis" is a term borrowed from Freud which Taylor in *Tears* uses to depict his own endeavor of writing the "limit."

43. This critique might be more pertinent to *Tears* than to earlier writings. For example, in *Erring*, Taylor embraces Nietzsche's "joyous affirmation of the play of the world and of the innocence of becoming" (168) that erases the guilt of unhappy consciousness. The gentle "eros" of such "second innocence" recedes in the growing gale of "tears" in later writings.

44. Sharon Welch, *Communities of Resistance and Solidarity: a Feminist Theology of Liberation* (Maryknoll, N.Y.: Orbis, 1985.) and *A Feminist Ethic of Risk* (Minneapolis: Fortress Press, 1990).

45. See chapter 2 of Welch, *A Feminist Ethic of Risk*.

46. Ibid., 114.

47. Included in Welch's critique are the liberal theories of

Alistair MacIntyre, Stanley Hauerwas, Jurgen Habermas, H. R. Niebuhr, and Paul Tillich.

48. This notion of a "mystification of relations of domination" was first proposed by Mary Daly in *Beyond God the Father: Toward a Philosophy of Women's Liberation* (Boston: Beacon Press, 1973).

49. E.g., on page 137 of *A Feminist Ethic of Risk*, Welch links the body with desire and sets this over against a neutral, disinterested reason that has no body.

50. Ibid., 138.

51. Ibid., 167.

52. Ibid., 178.

53. Ibid., 96 and 175.

54. Nietzsche, *Thus Spoke Zarathustra*, 105.

55. Ibid., 105.

56. See my 1991 American Academy of Religion presentation entitled, "Body as (Ex)tension or (Re)tension: From 'Serpentine Wanderer' to 'La Mère qui jouit' "—a comparison of the work of Taylor and Kristeva, which attempts to delineate and appraise some features of Kristeva's aesthetics.

57. Nietzsche, *Thus Spoke Zarathustra*, 76.

CHAPTER TWO

From Body as Phenomenal Field to Flesh as Field of Being

This world which is the same for all, no god, no man has made it, but it was always, is now and is forever an eternally living fire.

—Heraclitus, *Fragments*

Introduction

Few today would dispute the claim that the philosophical enterprise, as practiced in Western culture from the days of the pre-Socratics to our own, is a quest. And furthermore, in contrast to other disciplines which have a well-defined and circumscribed object of study, the quest of philosophy has traditionally been directed toward the "ground" of thinking, that which calls for reflection and culminates in the more specialized enterprises of the human and natural sciences.

The legacy of Nietzsche for the philosophies of body presented in this study is his unmasking of the dominant form of the philosophical quest, that is, traditional metaphysics, as girded in practices and relations of violence. For Nietzsche, the form of the "will-to-truth" which seeks a truth that is constant, unitary, and universal, attains this truth only through a violation of that which changes, is non-unitary, and particular. Therefore, the philosophical quest which has as its goal the certainty of an immutable truth is not only problematic epistemologically, as demonstrated by Kant, but even more seriously,

22

is problematic as a conceptual structure girded in violations of the sensual, of that realm subject to the limitations of time and space, of that which is contingent and transitory. Traditional metaphysics is both a violation of the body, and a covering over or mystification of this violation.

As articulated by those twentieth-century heirs of Nietzsche mentioned in the previous chapter, the exposure of the violence intrinsic to traditional metaphysics cannot be accomplished in the name of some greater truth, more unitary and universal than its predecessors. For these "greater truths," still caught within the same structure of reference as the prior ones, continue the project of metaphysics in its propensity both for representation and for domination. Put in theological terms, an unmasking of classical metaphysics in the name of a modernist metaphysic simply replaces the God of classical theism with the hollow idols of modernity.

Therefore, Nietzsche's cry on behalf of the body is not simply an unmasking of traditional metaphysics but even more, an "unmasking of unmasking." In the words of Gianni Vattimo:

> In Nietzsche's philosophy there is, on the one hand, a sort of *summa* of the "unmaskings" of metaphysics that philosophy has proposed in the past century or so, from the Marxian critique of ideology to the Freudian discovery of the unconscious, by way of positivism and the birth of the "human sciences." But there is also, as more characteristic of and specific to his thought, a radical "unmasking of unmasking" according to which even the idea of a truth that reveals a masking, of the attempt and claim to reach a solid "ground" beyond ideologies and every form of false consciousness, is, precisely, still a "human, all too human" devotion, still a mask. If, as Nietzsche maintains, we must distrust metaphysics—that is to say, for him as for us, the belief in a stable structure of Being that governs becoming and gives meaning to knowledge and norms to conduct—it is finally not "on strict grounds of knowledge" . . . (in which) we would remain always still prisoner of another metaphysics, . . . perpetuating the game from which we wish to escape.[1]

If the unmasking of metaphysics cannot be accomplished through an appeal to another metaphysic, then such subversion must come from a non-metaphysical realm—not outside the structure of metaphysical thinking, but at its limits.

In the terminology of this study, to think the body as limit is an "un-author-ized transgression" with a double function. First, it is an "unmasking of unmasking," a subversion of traditional metaphysics without appeal to any fixed, unitary, universal truth. And second, because such subversion, in exposing the "faults" of metaphysics, reveals the structure's "sensuous remain(s)," then to think the body as limit is also an exploration of the refuse or remain(s) of metaphysical truths. Such thinking then is not a new nihilism—not the collapse of all "will-to-truth" into either debilitating despair or Dionysiac intoxication. Instead, it is the spur to a vigorous ethical and theological thinking that gives voice to modes of relatedness other than those of violence and domination. To think the body as limit does not lead to a new fixed truth, but to new ways of being and dwelling on the earth—ways that are pluralistic, context dependent, and nonabusive of the "other."

Although the dominant form of the Western philosophical "will-to-truth" has been the quest for a stable and certain ground, it has not been the only form. As far back as Heraclitus, the philosophical quest was beckoned by an ultimately undefinable, elusive "logos." Closer to our own time, Heidegger, especially in his later writings, shows how traditional metaphysics manifests itself in *Ge-stell*, in the controlling and enframing mechanisms of modern technology. His appeal to "Being" as that which calls forth thinking is in large part an exposure of the violations of a metaphysics tied to technologies of destruction as well as an appeal for a nonrepresentational thinking that would resist such violations.[2]

Merleau-Ponty also rejects the curtailment of the philosophical quest to the representational thinking of traditional metaphysics. Philosophy for him is a mode of interrogation of the ground of thinking, but this ground, by resisting the objectification of Enlightenment forms of idealism and realism, is less a stable foundation for meaning than a lure to new ways of "being-in-the-world." For Merleau-Ponty, questioning originates in a stance of "wonder at the face of the world,"[3] a world not reducible to our representations. Wonder then is the originary question which gives philosophical reflection its limit and its lure. Put poetically, through wonder, one can perceive "the forms of transcendence (of being-in-the-world) fly up like sparks from a fire."[4]

This chapter presents the philosophy of Maurice Merleau-Ponty as a transitional position between the "objectified thinking" of the eighteenth and nineteenth centuries and the post-phenomenology and poststructuralism of Michel Foucault and Julia Kristeva. Our interest in Merleau-Ponty's philosophy of body stems from two strengths within his work. The first is his movement from the "objectified thinking" of the Enlightenment to an "aesthetics of lived existence," initially based on Husserl's phenomenology and Saussure's structuralism, but eventually moving beyond both of these. In such a "body aesthetics," the exclusionary opposition of subject/object relations of traditional metaphysics is overcome, thereby providing the rationale and impetus for the turn to post-phenomenological and poststructuralist notions of body relations. The first major contribution of Merleau-Ponty to our study is his articulation of the reasons for this turn.

Second, and of equal importance, Merleau-Ponty's phenomenology of body is a relational mode of "being-in-the-world," incorporating the challenges of a personal ethic as well as those posed by social and political realities of his day. Therefore, Merleau-Ponty, more than Heidegger, keeps at the forefront of his concerns the ethical implications of "body relations," particularly as these relations are impacted by oppressive forms of government, whether capitalist or socialist. Thinking this body then cannot be confused either with quietism or with more overt forms of complicity with abusive social and political power.

In turning to Merleau-Ponty's work, there are at least two phases of his philosophical quest that are pertinent to this study. The first one, presented in the *Phenomenology of Perception*, is his exploration of body as a conceptualization of the self/world relation which posed an alternative to the realism and idealism of his day. Refuting the ideas of "sensation" posited by empiricists as well as those of "conception" or "judgment" posited by "intellectualists" or idealists, Merleau-Ponty develops an aesthetic of the "lived body" as an operation of intentionality against the backdrop of ambiguity. The phenomenology of perception then retains a type of subjectivity that resists the privatization and certainty of Descartes' "cogito," Kant's architectonic of the mind, as well as Husserl's "transcendental ego." But in order to bring such a radically different subject to articulation, philosophy must plunge into the texture of the corporeal world. For Merleau-Ponty in his early writings, this entailed an examination of the experiences of people with bodily disorders.

The second phase of Merleau-Ponty's work, covering the period from 1955 to his death in 1961, is both internally diverse and far reaching in its attempt to meet the challenges of linguistic theory and politics in regard to the "body/subject." To address these challenges, he moves away from his investigation of psychiatric patients to an exploration of the creative process as experienced by artists, especially painters. Of importance here are his works, *Adventures of the Dialectic, Signs,* "Eye and Mind," and the text compiled posthumously from his last notes, *The Visible and the Invisible.*[5] By interweaving questions of language, politics, and art, Merleau-Ponty moves to the horizons of phenomenology and structuralism, thereby opening up a suggestive space for post-phenomenological and poststructuralist positions. Within this second phase, the concept of "perception" shifts to that of "bodily vision," "intentionality" shifts to "reversibility," and the natural "body" of the phenomenal field shifts to the chiasmic "flesh" of the field of Being.

The final section of this chapter will summarize Merleau-Ponty's contribution to the unmasking of metaphysics and exploration of its remain(s). For Merleau-Ponty, "objective thinking" is a form of metaphysics that violates the "lived experiences" and self/world relations of beings by reducing them to the representations of empiricism and idealism. His appeal to body and flesh as the "aesthesiological" medium of human becoming draws attention to the nonrepresentable conditions of "being-in-the-world." In giving voice to Merleau-Ponty's interrogation of these "limit conditions," we will be challenged to think the remain(s) of metaphysics as historical phenomena, that is, as flesh made visible in language and power. Merleau-Ponty's legacy then is not only his own questions and arenas of investigation, but also the new horizons of interrogation to which these lead. This chapter will conclude with ways in which Merleau-Ponty's own questions call for further exploration as well as ways in which they open up new questions left "unthought" within phenomenology and structuralism.

Body as Phenomenal Field

The empiricism of scientific realism is often regarded as anti-thetical to the intellectualism of continental idealism, and to some extent, rightfully so.[6] For empiricism, the subject is a passive recipient of sensation—the impact of causally related objects upon an objectified being. The subject thereby loses its subjectivity in being regarded solely as the site upon which the impact of external objects is registered.

Over against this "non-subject" is the privatized subject of idealism—an internal absolute consciousness, only acciden-tally related to the external world as the projection of objects for itself. Thus, while empircism diminishes or even eliminates human subjectivity by regarding the subject as one object causally related to other objects, idealism creates an autono-mous subject, immune to the influences of the material world except as a mechanized extension of itself, subservient to its own projects and needs.

What holds these otherwise antithetical perspectives in tandem is their attitude toward the material world as a realm of objects, explicit in themselves and causally related. In the words of Merleau-Ponty,

We started off from a world in itself which acted upon our eyes so as to cause us to see it, and we now have consciousness of a thought about the world, but the nature of this world remains unchanged: it is still defined by the absolute mutual exteriority of its parts, and is merely duplicated throughout its extent by a thought which sustains it. We pass from absolute objectivity to absolute subjectivity, but this second idea is no better than the first.[7]

Over against the "objective thought" of empiricism and ideal-ism alike is the "phenomenology of perception," perception which begins with a subject already embedded in the ebb and flow of the world, situated within the "phenomenal field" of one's own body as well as the body of natural and cultural relationships. The phenomenology of perception begins with the facticity of "being-in-the-world."[8]

For some interpreters of Merleau-Ponty's body philosophy as depicted in his early work, body is understood primarily as an ambiguous entity, operating within the overlapping and complex ambiguities of the phenomenal field. For others, body is understood primarily as a mode of intentionality—a radicalizing of Husserl's project and yet in continuity with it.[9] Without denying the value of both emphases, my own analysis will focus on body as an aesthetic which holds in tension the intentionality of a "body/subject" against the backdrop of a radically temporalized and spatialized existence.

My rationale for emphasizing the aesthetic of body is twofold. First, Merleau-Ponty himself, following the writing of the *Phenomenology of Perception*, turned to art as a genre capable of depicting the dynamic he was trying to express through his concept of perception. Thus, one might regard the aesthetic as part of Merleau-Ponty's "unthought thought" in this early stage, just as Merleau-Ponty himself spoke of drawing upon the "unthought thought" of Husserl's *Fifth Meditation*.[10]

The second reason for emphasizing body as an aesthetic is its suggestiveness for moral philosophy. Terry Eagleton, highly skeptical of modern forms of the aesthetic due to their alliance with capitalist ideology, still recognizes the power and potential of an aesthetic of the body which operates as a counterforce to dominant ideologies. His stated goal in *The Ideology of the Aesthetic* could also be said of Merleau-Ponty—the goal of reuniting "the idea of body with more traditional political topics of the state . . . through the mediatory category of the aesthetic."[11] A postmodern "aesthetics of body" that resists the totalizing impulses of modernist aesthetics has the potential of subverting the values intrinsic to subject/object dualism, thereby opening a space for a radically alternative "ontology of relatedness." That is the goal of this chapter and of this study as a whole.

Turning again to the body as phenomenal field, we will proceed by looking at this field from two directions, that is, from the perspective of a "body/subject" perceiving the world and then from the perspective of the world interacting with the "body/subject." Traditionally, these two perspectives have been posed as two alternative sets of relationships, that is, those internal to objects or "things-in-themselves," and those between the subject and objectified world. As we shall see from closer inspection of the phenomenal field, any firm dichotomy between "in-itself" and "for-itself" relations is part of the problem of dualistic thinking, thinking which Merleau-Ponty trys to overcome.[12] Such relations are for him on a continuum, but by looking at this continuum from its two poles of "subject" and "world," the aesthetics of their relationship becomes clearer.

The first perspective then, from the "inside," shows the "body/subject" as internally differentiated and enigmatic, both present and absent to itself, both subject and object. To support this, Merleau-Ponty gives what have become two of his best-known examples—that of a "phantom limb" and that of "two-hands-touching."

In the first example, both the empiricist and the idealist have difficulty explaining the phenomenon of a person continuing to experience an arm after it has been severed from his/ her body. For the empiricist, for whom the body is a composite of molecular substances and causal processes, a phantom limb is a failure of the subject's perception, a failure effected through the suppression of sensations that would inform the person of the truth of the matter.[13] When the notion of body is wedded to the physiological explanation of "objective thought," a severed arm is totally absent from the body. It has no presence. In contrast, for the idealist, for whom the body is an extension of the subject's projects through representation, the phantom limb is a "memory" or "positive judgment" based on consciousness. Due to the primacy of concepts over percepts in this perspective, the arm in its presence to consciousness has no absence.[14]

In both perspectives, Merleau-Ponty argues, "we are imprisoned in the categories of the objective world, in which there is no middle term between presence and absence."[15] For him, the arm is neither primarily the source of sensation nor the object of representation, but part of one's "bodily scheme" or way of "being-in-the-world."

> To have a phantom arm is to remain open to all the actions of which the arm alone is capable; it is to retain the practical field which one enjoyed before mutilation. The body is the vehicle of being in the world, and having a body is, for a living creature, to be intervolved in a definite environment, to identify oneself with certain projects and be continually committed to them.[16]

If then the body is neither simply a material substance nor an extension of consciousness, but a way of "being-in-the-world," then a phantom limb is an "absent presence" or a "present absence." In bringing to remembrance one's habitual tacit relations within the world, the arm is present—it continues to exist as the medium through which one maintains a certain mode of relationality.[17] Yet, at the same time, in the limb's failure to continue to uphold these relations in the same way following mutilation, the arm is absent. That is, when the phantom arm is no long able to "remain open to all the actions of which the arm alone is capable," the practical field of one's habitual actions shifts to close down certain potentials and open up others. In losing its ability for certain types of action in the world, the arm is absent.

In being a "present absence" or "absent presence," the phantom limb suggests the aesthetic of the body itself, that is, the tensions between one's tacit knowledge of habitual relations with the world—what Merleau-Ponty calls "threads of intentionality" directed outward from the body—[18]and the "remainder" or "supplement" that appears prior to and external to these intentions and arouses new thoughts and volitions.[19] The aesthetic of the body then is the ongoing tension between habitual modes of relatedness and the "remainder" of these relations in an ever shifting, ever moving phenomenal field. This is the "aesthetic of body" from the perspective of the subject.

Following on the heels of this discussion of the "phantom arm," Merleau-Ponty continues his polemic against "objective thought" with another example of a disabled person—this time someone who sustained brain damage from an exploding shell during World War I. Here again, by examining the nature of the disability and the failure of empiricists and idealists alike to address it adequately, Merleau-Ponty shifts his focus to the "bodily scheme" of habit, practical knowledge, and intentionality.[20]

Despite initial appearances, Merleau-Ponty, in using these examples, is not developing a philosophy of "abnormal body." Instead, these abnormalities function to bring to the foreground the normal operation of any "body/subject" in the world. In order to make this point, he alludes to the skills of typing, driving, and playing a musical instrument—all modes of tacit interaction with the world. In each case, the instrument of the activity becomes, like the arm or like the blind person's stick, part of the body as a vehicle of intentionality toward the world.[21]

In order to focus on the "present absence" of *all* "body/subjects" and, at the same time, give a fuller account of intentionality, we turn to the second example alluded to earlier—that of "two-hands-touching." When "I touch my right hand with my left," says Merleau-Ponty, "my right hand, as an object, has the strange property of being able to feel too." Thus, a double sensation is created, that of being both subject (touching) and object (being touched) at the same time in the same body.[22]

Empiricists deal with this phenomenon by creating a distinct category of experience, the "kinaesthetic," based on an hypothesized inner "psyche"—itself an object of scientific investigation. But Merleau-Ponty finds this solution artificial and unsatisfying. Instead of creating special categories tied to the myths of "objective thought," one can see, he says, how "two-hands-touching" reveals the inner ambiguity of the body. More specifically, it reveals an intentionality of one hand as an aiming toward the other in practical action without ever creating an identity with the other. There is a "gap," an "écart," between the touching and the touched—a gap which Merleau-Ponty will later develop as the "abyss" between the visibles of the world.[23] What suffices at present though in depicting the aesthetic of the "body//subject" is that this gap is not a barrier to knowledge, but is instead the transcendence of the object that both resists being possessed by the subject and yet calls for further interaction. "Intentionality" for Merleau-Ponty is an "intentional arc," a spanning of subject and object in the practical field of action, but a spanning which always incorporates a "difference." This "difference" or transcendence of the "touched" to the "touching" is both the limit to our knowledge and its lure. The sirens of knowledge are in the "difference."

In addressing the "touching" and "touched" of the "intentional arc," we have already moved from the vantage point of the "body/subject" to that of the world. What then is this pole of "world," this realm of things and subjects outside of the "body/subject"? In the very asking of this question, a problem arises because, for Merleau-Ponty, the world is never completely *outside of* the "body/subject." Just as the "hand being touched" does not exist "in-itself" outside of the phenomenal field of body, so too the world outside of the physical body does not exist "in-itself" outside of the "lived body" of motility or action. That is, the subject-world continuum is held together by the shared existential structures and dimensions of space and time. Therefore, there is no "world-in-itself" outside of these structures. "The thing and the world," says Merleau-Ponty, "exist only in so far as they are experienced by me or by subjects like me."[24] There is no world unrelated to the "body/subject."

Yet this assertion, that the world is necessarily related to a subject, is from the vantage point of "objective thought" an argument tied to an idealist position. From this position, the world is a kind of Kantian idea, no longer, for Merleau-Ponty, dependent upon the projections of a thinking subject, but still dependent upon the "intentional threads" of the existential structures of the "body/subject." World then remains an extension of the subject, not Descartes' and Kant's subjects of constituting minds, but the "body/subject" of habitual action.

Although Merleau-Ponty tries to counteract this reduction of world to the subject by continually reminding us of the "insurpassable plentitude" of the world as "something transcendent standing in the wake of subjectivity,"[25] he does not fully escape the confines of the philosophies of consciousness in this respect.[26] Eventually, in his later writings, he sheds the remaining traces of idealism implicit within his notion of intentionality and challenges the presupposition of a subject's experiential "structures of existence" as being the site for knowledge. However, in the *Phenomenology*, the world, although always transcendent to the perceptions of the "body/subject," is not transcendent to the existential structures of the subject. Put otherwise, the world, like the "hand-being-touched," is itself subject and object, present and absent, but with a subjectivity and presence always qualified and circumscribed by the existential structures of the "body/subject." In the phenomenal field of the body's perception, the world is more dependent upon the subject than vice versa. Therefore, although the subject/object relations of "objective thought" have here been dealt a serious blow, it is not fatal. Subject/object relations, along with the values intrinsic to them, have not yet been fully overcome.

We will return to this dependence of world on the subject in our exploration of Merleau-Ponty's second philosophical phase, but before proceeding to that, there remains one final aspect of the subject-world continuum which deserves our attention. That is the effects of subject-world interrelatedness as a "coming to expression" of both subject and world.

Alluding to a wordplay in French between "connaissance" (knowledge) and "co-naissance" (co-birth),[27] Merleau-Ponty presents the dynamic interrelatedness of "body/subject" and "world" as a process through which both poles come to articulation or, in his words, "come to expression." As discussed earlier, the gap or "écart" between subject and object for Merleau-Ponty is a space of plentitude, a sediment of powers and possibilities which are called forth in the dynamic of the "touched" and the "touching." Therefore for him, "coming to expression" presupposes neither the "bruta facta" of empiricism nor the constituting thoughts of an autonomous subject. Indeed, expression is not secondary to nor derivative of any prior substance, essence or idea. Instead, it is a process of "ekstase," a dynamic in which both "body/subject" and "world," as projects of each other, call forth the other as the "movement of transcendence" between them.[28]

The relation of "body/subject" to "world," and particularly that of subject to other subjects in the world, can be depicted as a "present absence" or "absent presence." The "others" of the world are present to the subject in that they "exist only to the extent that [the subject] takes them up and lives them."[29] At the same time, these "others" always transcend the subject's intentions and through that absence create an absence of the subject to him/herself. They thereby throw the subject outside (ek-stasis) of him/herself. The crux of philosophy, says Merleau-Ponty, is to show "how the presence to myself ('Urprasenz') which establishes my own limits and conditions every alien presence is at the same time depresentation ('Entgegenwärtigung') and throws me outside myself."[30]

Through the intermingling of body and world both come to expression, and for Merleau-Ponty, the primary example of this is speech. Once again, his own alternative is developed in juxtaposition to two others: that of empiricist and mechanistic psychologies and that of intellectualist or idealist ones. For the empiricist, the "word" is the result of stimuli or states of mind operating according to fixed laws of neurological mechanics.[31] For the idealist, the "word" is simply the external sign of an internal categorial operation, the "external accompaniment of thought."[32] In neither case does the "word" itself have meaning.

In the first [case] there is nobody to speak; in the second, there is certainly a subject, but a thinking one, not a speaking one. As far as speech is concerned, intellectualism is hardly any different from empiricism . . . since [for both] the word is a passive shell. Thus we refute both intellectualism and empiricism by simply saying that "the word has a meaning."[33]

What then is this meaning that "inhabits" words and "is inseparable from them"?[34] It is for Merleau-Ponty an "existential meaning," a manifestation or revelation of one's living relation with oneself and with others.[35] As such, language for Merleau-Ponty is neither purely natural nor merely conventional. It is natural in that it is a gesture of the body and does not exist apart from the body. At the same time, it is conventional in that it is drawn from the sedimentations of culture, themselves the "surplus of our existence over natural being."[36] But just as body cannot be reduced either to "natural processes" or to "mental and cultural representation," so too the speech of Merleau-Ponty's "speaking subject" is neither merely natural nor conventional but rather an expression of "relations-in-the-world," relations spawned within the ambiguities of the phenomenal field.

Speech for Merleau-Ponty is a wave in the sea of existence. This sea, having no foundation other than itself, still continually gathers itself in waves, hurtling itself beyond its own limits.[37] Neither expressing a foundational substance or thought, nor being limited to a unidirectional intention of subject to object, the wave of speech is the upsurge of the multi-directional and moving currents of existence. Like the emergence of gesture from "the unco-ordinated movements of infancy" or "the emergence of love from desire," speech is an expression of the "co-naissance" of subject and world. It is the miracle of their coexistence.[38]

This concludes our exploration of the aesthetic of body as phenomenal field set forth in Merleau-Ponty's early writing. Through his attentiveness to the experiences of people with bodily disorders, Merleau-Ponty succeeded in veering away from the "objective thinking" of empiricism and idealism. The tacit relations of the "body/subject" defy the reductionism of subjectivity either to the effects of external stimuli or to the operations of an autonomous mind. Furthermore, Merleau-

Ponty moves toward an "ontology of relatedness" between the "body/subject" and "others" of the world, culminating in an ontology which avoids the solipsism of Cartesian egos as well as the fusion of selves in Bergsonian intuitionism. His own alternative is based on the "ek-stases" which occur through the "gap" or "écart" of the transcendence of a body in its relations to itself as well as to others. Although these "ek-stases" occur in the actions of diverse kinds of body gestures, including those of sexuality, the primary arena of expression is that of speech. For Merleau-Ponty, a subject comes to articulation in the praxis of language.

In this early work, Merleau-Ponty provides pointers toward a position which overcomes the problematics of subject/object relations. Yet, as indicated in his own writing, he does not initially succeed in this endeavor. This shortcoming can in part be attributed to the language which Merleau-Ponty uses to depict his own alternative. Words like "intentionality," "expression," and "perception" are usually associated with the kind of metaphysics that Merleau-Ponty is trying to overcome. Like Heidegger, he struggles with a questioning of the subject that challenges the structures of a metaphysics of subjectivity, and yet finds himself in his own language usage, still caught within its confines.[39]

Furthermore, aside from limitations posed by the conventional meaning of certain words, Merleau-Ponty is still focused on the subject instead of focusing on the fabric of relatedness within which the subject is an intersection of forces. There are in the argument of the *Phenomenology* forces within the currents of existence which prompt an upsurge into "waves of expression," but these are not fully explored. In shifting from body as phenomenal field to flesh as field of Being, Merleau-Ponty is not deserting the insights of his early work, but pushing them to a deeper interrogation—from the phenomenology of perception to the ontology of the field of Being. It is to this second phase that we now turn.

Chiasmic Flesh as Field of Being

In a note dated July 1959, less than two years before his death, Merleau-Ponty speaks of a shift in his philosophical quest. "The problems posed in the *Phenomenology of Perception*," he

says, "are insoluble because I start there from the "conscious-
ness-object" distinction."[40] Logically prior to this division into
subject/object, even revised as body/subject and world, is the
ontological question of the "visible" or the "there is" ("il y a").
Thus, while the phenomenology of perception takes up the
questions of existence within the metaphysical framework of
dualism, Merleau-Ponty, in his later writing, tries to overcome
this framework by returning to the originating events of the
"there is."

In doing so, it is still the sensible world that solicits the
philosopher's gaze, but with a new twist. Instead of focusing
on speaking, feeling, and touching subjects, Merleau-Ponty
now asks "*what*, across the successive and simultaneous community of speaking subjects, 'wishes,' 'speaks,' and finally
'thinks'?"[41] What is this flesh or "there is" which is logically
prior to the differentiations of particular patterns of subjectivity? What causes subjects to emerge and then speaks through
them? What are the powers of the flesh which surge forth
into shapes, colors, and sounds—calling for expression in the
human through painting, speaking, and thinking?

In pursuit of these questions, Merleau-Ponty begins again
with a warning. In the *Phenomenology*, it was "objective
thinking" which was the target of his critique. But now, in
asking about the "what" that "thinks" through the subject, the
questioning shifts to those prejudicative modes of relating—
those modes of the body's tacit dimensions prior to thinking,
that is, those of touching and seeing. Thus, the warning of
these later writings is directed toward a truncated and dis-
torted way of seeing the world. Merleau-Ponty begins with a
critique of the "gaze of the spectator."

The spectator, oblivious to her or his situatedness in the
midst of the fabric of existence makes two serious errors in
interpreting the world. First, she or he claims a position of
neutrality, an "eagle-eye view" supposedly untouched by the
flesh that it observes. Second, the spectator, due to this high-
altitude vantage point, claims to discover within the vicissitudes of its representations, stable structures or essences to
serve as a foundation for meaning. Thus, "there is established
a philosophy which knows neither difficulties nor problems
nor paradoxes nor reversals . . . [only] the truth of my life,
which is also the truth of the world and of the other lives."[42]

Such was the enterprise of Rene Descartes along with his train of positivistic offspring.

Yet in exploring the phenomenon of seeing prior to the imposition of this dualistic grid on the flesh of the world, one understands seeing in a radically different way. First, as an almost banal observation, seeing is always partial. The seer neither sees one's own back nor the far side of the objects she/he observes. All seeing is perspectival. There is no neutral vantage point and no totalizing vision. But while some interpreters of the world stop there, stuck in a relativism of competing perspectives, Merleau-Ponty is not satisfied with this. Instead, he pushes toward an "ontology" of seeing, an alternative to all absolutes, including that of absolute relativism. And it is in the casting of this alternative—that of the "gaze of the body"—wherein he makes his most important contribution.

The "body/seer," located in the middle of the "there is," is at the same time seeing and being seen. As such, analogous to the experience of "two-hands-touching," the seer not only realizes a "present absence" in her/himself but in the "seen" as well. There is a depth dimension to the "seen," a dimension effected by the overlapping or coiling over of the visible upon the visible. And what this dimension reveals to the seer is the interrelatedness of the visible with the invisible in the flesh of the world. Over against all positivisms which posit total presence as a condition for meaning, as well as all philosophies of "negativity" which posit total absence,[43] Merleau-Ponty argues for a "present absence" or "visible invisible" in the flesh of the world which are not in opposition to each other but necessary correlates in the emergence of meaning.

One example of this intertwining of the visible and the invisible is revealed in the experience of painters. The blank or "empty" spaces in a painting are just as important as the painted ones for giving space and coloration to the whole. In the water colors of Cezanne, for example, "space . . . radiates around planes that cannot be assigned to any place at all."[44] Such "empty" spaces are in a sense the medium through which the picture comes to be, the inscription of the invisible in the visible.

Meaning is "invisible," but the invisible is not the contradictory of the visible: the visible itself has an invisible inner framework ('membrure'), and the in-

visible is the secret counterpart of the visible, it appears
only within it, it is the "Nichturpräsentierbar" which is
presented to me as such within the world—one cannot
see it there and every effort to "see it there" makes it
disappear, but it is "in the line" of the visible, it is its
virtual focus, it is inscribed within it . . . the visible is
pregnant with the invisible.[45]

Illustrative of the role of the invisible in the emergence of
the visible for the "gaze of the body" is the example of the flesh
of the world as water in a pool with tiles at the bottom.

When through the water's thickness I see the tiling at
the bottom of a pool, I do not see it despite the water
and the reflections there; I see it through them and
because of them. If there were no distortions, no ripples
of sunlight, if it were without this flesh that I saw the
geometry of the tiles, then I would cease to see it as it is
and where it is—which is to say, beyond any identical,
specific place. I cannot say that the water itself—the
aqueous power, the sirupy and shimmering element—is in space; all this is not somewhere else either,
but it is not in the pool. It inhabits it, it materializes
itself there, yet it is not contained there; and if I raise
my eyes toward the screen of cypresses where the web
of reflections is playing, I cannot gainsay the fact that
the water visits it, too, or at least sends into it, upon it,
its active and living essence. This internal animation,
this radiation of the visible is what the painter seeks
under the name of depth, of space, of color.[46]

Like the fluids used by developers of photographic film, fluid
here is the medium within which the visibles come to be.

For Merleau-Ponty, seeing the world through one's body,
in this example, through the "flesh" of "ripples of sunlight in
water," is a truer seeing than the representations of the spectator. This attempt to divorce truth from representation becomes
even more evident in his next example—that of the truth of
painting over that of the supposed truth of a photograph.

When a horse is photographed at that instant when he
is completely off the ground, with his legs almost folded
under him—an instant, therefore, when he must be
moving—why does he look as if he were leaping in

place? Then why do Gericault's horses really "run" on canvas, in a posture impossible for a real horse at a gallop? It is just that the horses in "Epsom Derby" bring me to see the body's grip upon the soil and that, according to a logic of body and world I know well, these "grips" upon space are also ways of taking hold of time ("la durée"). Rodin said very wisely, "It is the artist who is truthful, while the photograph is mendacious; for, in reality, time never stops cold."[47]

The representation of the horse in the photograph destroys the overlapping of one visible on the other. The painting, by showing horses as having "a foot in each instant" retains the depth, the "radiation" of the flesh beyond itself. What is impossible to capture in the still frame of a photograph can yet be depicted by a painting that retains the truth of movement.

To summarize, the "gaze of the body" does not see the world as representation but as a "horizon-structure," a flesh of thickness and depth, created by the overlapping of the visible upon the visible, the inscription of the visible by the invisible, and the coiling over of the visible upon the seer. The world is never fully present to the seer; it always retains an absence or hiddenness which defies full explication. Yet this absence is itself not a void, but the lining of the visible, that which in the aesthetics of flesh brings the visible to expression.

One is reminded here of the "phantom arm" of the *Phenomenology* which served as a medium for the body/subject's actions in the practical field of relations. The "flesh" of this later formulation is also a medium of practical knowledge. It also has a "present absence" or "visible invisible" character, and it also operates within a dynamic field of relations constituted by gaps between visibles. And yet, the flesh does not have the limitations of the "phantom arm." The flesh is not an existential dimension of the subject, but is rather the prejudicative milieu in which all subjectivity comes to expression. Furthermore, the flesh is not traversed by the intentionality of a "tacit cogito" but by the forces of "wild" or "brute Being." It is to this ontological aspect of flesh as a field of forces that we now give more concerted attention.

There are several ways in which Merleau-Ponty explores the forces that traverse the "thickness of the flesh," bringing forth the visibles of the world. One which occurs frequently throughout his work is that of flesh as an element, that is, as something "midway between the spatio-temporal individual and the idea, a sort of incarnate principle that brings a style of being wherever there is a fragment of being."[48] As such, flesh is neither matter nor mind nor substance. It is neither a fact nor a sum of facts but the "facticity" which makes the fact a fact. It is the "aesthesiological principle" of all being.

For the ancient Greeks, the elements consisted of air, water, fire, and soil. In depicting the depth of the visible, we have already referred to the positive role of water in seeing the tiles and trees of the world. Perhaps even more illustrative of the forces traversing the flesh is the element of fire. For here, we have a causation internal to the flesh, a spark which leaps from the "depths of the visible" to the seer, inciting the painter's vision. Quoting from a book on the artist Paul Klee, Merleau-Ponty writes: "In the immemorial depth of the visible, something moved, caught fire, and engulfed his body: everything he paints is in answer to this incitement."[49]

What is true here for the visual arts is also true for the creative expressions of music, literature, even of language. Each comes about through a complicity of the seer and the seen, through what Merleau-Ponty calls a "reversibility" or "promiscuity of perception."[50] The visible is not simply "there," lined up against the wall for inspection. When Merleau-Ponty insists on the depth of the flesh, the inscription of the invisible on the visible, the "coiling over" of the visible on the seer, he is speaking of forces of the flesh, that is, powers of attraction or repulsion which are not in front of the seer's eyes as much as behind them, or better, in the lining of the seer's body. The visible lures the seer, even possesses her or him through one's mutual complicity in the depths of flesh.[51]

What is this "phantom" which seduces the seer to creative expression:[52] Although Merleau-Ponty, like the painter Klee, resists being "caught in immanence,"[53] he is especially careful in developing a type of transcendence to distinguish it from the transcendence of a long history of spectators. The "wild, brute Being" traversing the flesh of the world is not for Merleau-Ponty a transcendent Being, a "massive individual" external to the world through whom the world emerges.[54] Rather, "wild Being," as that "inalienable horizon" with which the seer is already circumvented, cannot be positively denoted, not only as an individual, but as any fact, substance, or essence. As the originating force of all visibles, "wild Being" is the "uncultivated" invisible, always logically prior to our schemes, eluding representation and possession.

And yet, such Being is "ontological" in that it is by virtue of such Being, by the "unmotivated upsurge of brute Being,"[55] that the field of Being explodes into the visibles of the world. There is a dehiscence of Being, a continual "unfolding by differentiation,"[56] open to the "perceptual faith" or "body gaze" of the philosopher or artist, indeed "spoken" through her or him. In such a way, Merleau-Ponty links Being to the body/subject, that through which Being "speaks."[57]

What then is the subject for Merleau-Ponty in these later writings? By his own admission, the "speaking subjects" of the *Phenomenology* did overcome the "objective thinking" of empiricism and idealism but stopped short of subverting the subject/object dichotomy of binary thinking. So there is a sense in which the "self" of his later writings is an extension of the earlier "speaking subjects" and yet also an attempt to reach beyond the limitations of their formulation.

Unfortunately, due to Merleau-Ponty's sudden death, the material we have on this alternative "self" is both brief and fragmentary, creating frustration in interpreting it with respect to its author but also intrigue in the openness of its possibilities. One clue to the type of selfhood being sought after by Merleau-Ponty in his last writings is his reference to the "nobody" of Ulysses. As expected from his rejection of a subjectivity of "full presence" in the *Phenomenology*, he is not interested in a subject of "something" or "somebody." Yet the antithesis to this, the idea of the self as "nobody," as a "nichtiges Nichts," as formulated by Sartre, having no essence prior to its radical self-constitution through decisions, is also not acceptable.[58] In this "nobody" self, hope is dependent upon the will of the subject to act rather than merely be acted upon. It is still tied to the "constituting acts" of modernist forms of subjectivity.

But the "nobody" of Ulysses is not a "nichtiges Nichts." There is a hiddenness in Ulysses' self. In fact, in the saga of the Odyssey, his hiddenness from the Cyclops is his salvation. But the hiddenness is only part of his selfhood; it is not absolute. In Merleau-Ponty's words, it is a "nothingness sunken into a local and temporal openness," that is, into vision and feeling.[59] Like a cavern harboring latent content and yet open to the world, or like a stage where the acts happen framed in darkness, the self has a presence, even an essence, but a presence or essence of vision and feeling that emerges out of and is sustained by the backdrop of "nothingness." Given that for Merleau-Ponty this "nothingness" is the invisible of Being, the self is not a "somebody," a full presence. Neither is it "nobody," a complete absence. Rather, it is the way in which Being manifests itself at one intersection of space and time. The "self" for Merleau-Ponty is an "ontological relief."[60]

But a self imaged as cavern can be misleading. Despite its plentitude of possibilities within and openness upon the world, a cavern is a static entity, lacking both subjectivity and intense interaction with other caverns. Something more needs to be said about the self in order to depict it not only as an "ontology of ambiguity," but also as an "ontology of relatedness." Merleau-Ponty does this by returning to the metaphor of "two-hands-touching."

In the *Phenomenology*, the image of hands "touching-being-touched" was used primarily in reference to the two hands of one person, depicting the body as itself both subject and object, as internally ambiguous. In his later work, Merleau-Ponty doesn't desert these insights, but extends them to the wider arena of interhuman relations. In his words, "If my left hand can touch my right hand while it palpates the tangibles, can touch it touching, can turn its palpation back upon it, why, when touching the hand of another, would I not touch in it the same power to espouse the things that I have touched in my own?"[61] As Merleau-Ponty knows, this supposedly innocent question is implicated in a long conversation within philosophies of consciousness called the problem of other minds. If one begins, as Descartes did, with a world dependent upon an autonomous, thinking being, then events of the body such as "two-hands-touching" belong to "one sole space of consciousness."[62] From within this solipsistic space, there is no way to touch an "other" as "other," only as an extension of one's own self.

But the unity of Merleau-Ponty's "body/self" is not an "autonomous consciousness." In his early work, the unity of the self was posited through the "existential dimensions" of the subject, dependent upon a "tacit cogito." Later, in *The Visible and the Invisible*, Merleau-Ponty breaks away from both of these idealist positions by positing the unity of the self as an "identity of difference and difference," an identity ignited by the sparks of transcendence between self and "other" within the fabric of "intercorporeal" relations. These relations, now understood as fully reversible, open the self to a "domain of the visible and the tangible, *which extends further than the things I touch and see at present*," that is, the domain of Being.[63] The self of the flesh is radically relational, constituted by a relatedness to the "other" in which the other is not an extension of one's own inner consciousness or ego, internal to the self. Nor is it an "alter ego" fully external to the self. Rather, the "other" is a trace of the self, the outside of the self's inside and the inside of its outside together creating the friction that ignites the sparks of human becoming.

The notion of selfhood that Merleau-Ponty hints at in his early work and then expands upon later is the "decentered self." In the concluding remarks of the *Phenomenology*, Merleau-Ponty refers to a process of "depresentation" of the self in its interaction with the "other." Taking this up again in his later work, he reiterates the notion that such "depresentation," now called "decentering," is not annihilation of the self, but the way in which a self moves toward its own identity.[64] Such "decentering" is neither a dialectic between self and other in which interaction occurs between two discrete entities nor is it a fusion. In resisting both of these options, Merleau-Ponty moves toward the third alternative of an aesthetics of relationality, that is, of an alterity of relatedness within the concrete fields of history and culture.[65]

Usually for Merleau-Ponty, the "decentering" of the self by the "other," including not just other selves but the otherness of the world of all natural and cultural entities, has a positive cast. Not only does the gaze of the body "caress the things . . . espous[ing] their contours and their reliefs,"[66] the things or others in turn "touch" the self, evoking responses of astonishment, ecstasy, and inspiration. One gets a feel for this aspect of "intercorporeality" in the following passage:

> The body . . . clasps another body, applying [itself to it] carefully with its whole extension, forming tirelessly with its hands the strange statue which in its turn gives everything it receives; the body is lost outside of the world and its goals, fascinated by the unique occupation of floating in Being with another life, of

making itself the outside of its inside and the inside of its outside. And henceforth movement, touch, vision, applying themselves to the other and to themselves, return toward their source and, in the patient and silent labor of desire, begin the paradox of expression.[67]

This is one dimension of the "coiling over of the visible upon the visible," one not foreign to the sensibilities of the French.

There is another dimension of the self-other relation though, only hinted at by Merleau-Ponty, and that is a decentering of the self through "transgression" or encroachment of the other, a decentering by assault. At times, Merleau-Ponty seems to attribute this type of decentering to the spectator, for it is the "gaze of the spectator" which like a judge "elevated above all contestation without place, without relativities, faceless like an obsession" has the power to "crush me with a glance."[68] This is a gaze explored with a vengeance by Foucault, the theorist of our next chapter.

And yet, even the "other" with a face, the "other" of the flesh, calls the self into question through confrontation, evoking a self as a "unity by transgression or by correlative encroachment."[69] This is not the annihilation or rape of spectator relations, but neither is it "floating in Being with another life." One is then left with questions about such transgression. What are transgressive relations at the level of interpersonal relationships? What are they at the social/political level? Does transgression include the "ek-stasis" of the artist and the lover? If so, how? And what other "body relations" are transgressive? How, for example does one differentiate between the encroachment of a transgressive body, and the annihilation of a spectator? What are the differences between an "ontology of the flesh" and an "ontology of spectators"? Furthermore, how does transgression fit with the event of the "wave of Being"? What are its theological implications?

These, of course, cannot all be addressed through the fragmentary remarks of Merleau-Ponty's last writings. Yet these writings do act as vectors for the posing of these issues and for their further interrogation. And the arena which they point to as a gathering place for further reflection is that of language and power. As a conclusion to this section on flesh as field of Being, we offer Merleau-Ponty's tentative formulations within this historical arena.

An Historicizing of "Flesh" as Language and Power

From the time of his earliest writings, language was a concern for Merleau-Ponty, but a concern that underwent several important shifts. Because the interest of this study is on the movement of his thought from the aesthetics of the phenomenal body to those of the flesh, we will confine our discussion to two approaches to language found in Merleau-Ponty's work, from language as the "speech" or "expression" of the body/subject to language as articulations of the flesh. And power, although not given much explicit attention by Merleau-Ponty, is closely associated with the operations of language and will be treated here as such.

As presented earlier in this study, Merleau-Ponty in the *Phenomenology* presented language as the expression of the "co-naissance" of subject and world. For him, this expression did not arise from the causal relations of external stimuli nor from the inner operations of thought. Instead, the spoken word had its own meaning, a meaning surging forth from waves of existence, that is, from the existential dimensions of a "body/subject-in-the-world."

The difference between this understanding of language and the one emerging in his later work is analogous to the difference between the "phantom arm" and the flesh.[70] In the earlier formulation, Merleau-Ponty develops "the speaking subject." In the later one, he shifts to the "speaking world."[71] In the earlier one, speech is a product of the "co-naissance" between body/subject and world. In the later one, language is in some way prior to the self, taking form in the "deep-rooted relations of lived experience" and "called forth" in the articulations of the self, especially in those of literature and poetry.[72] In the earlier one, speech emerges out of the circularity between body/subject and world. In the later one, language has a futurity, an "openness" upon Being.[73]

The language of the "speaking world" then for Merleau-Ponty is an "operative language," not "the depository of fixed and acquired significations,"[74] not "a system of explicit relations between signs and signified, sounds and meaning,"[75] not the speech of a subject tied to the "tacit cogito." Like the flesh of the world, it has thickness and depth. Like the flesh, it is traversed by the forces of "wild Being" operating within the relations of social selves both through seduction and offense.[76] Like the flesh, language has an internal dynamic, an aesthetic through which the "visibles" of the world materialize and yet are not confined.[77]

And finally, although power is not a dominant theme for Merleau-Ponty, it does play a role in respect to language, a role which calls for further investigation. Although he doesn't use the word power in the *Phenomenology*, one could interpret his development of "expression" as power, the power of "co-birthing" within the relationship of subject to world. In *The Visible and the Invisible*, the concept of power is articulated as the "power of anticipation or of prepossession" of the self as the site for the "speaking" of "wild Being."[78] The power of language here is its ability to decenter the self through entice-ment or encroachment. It is the power of becoming through the dehiscence of Being within the significations of historical existence.

What then has Merleau-Ponty accomplished in his interro-gation of the "body/subject" and of the "flesh"? And where do these vectors of thinking lead? We began this chapter by situating his philosophy of body within a trajectory of thinking that originates in wonder. As we have witnessed in following this thread of his work, such wonder is not an excuse for passivity or basking in the "there is." For Merleau-Ponty, as for others before and after him in this trajectory, wonder initiates interrogation and drives the pursuit of meaning—if not to final answers, at least to deeper insights into the internal dynamics of the field of Being, this "aesthesiological" flesh within which we dwell.[79]

In the course of his own journey, Merleau-Ponty revealed modes of thinking within the modern West that have stultified relations among the entities of the Earth, fixing them in the oppositional categories of subject/object, and thereby sanction-ing modes of possession and annihilation intrinsic to "objec-tive thinking" and to the "gaze of the spectator." An alternative mapping of relationality—one which subverts this binary logic as it manifests itself throughout the social fabric, is desper-ately needed. And although Merleau-Ponty does not offer his own formulations as a final solution—in fact, admitting that no solution is final—he did open up new horizons for interroga-tion. He began with body as "bodily schema" or practical action in the world, and enlarged it to an investigation of artistic experience in order to examine the wider context and forces traversing the body, registered in the body's prejudicative modes of seeing and touching, and calling forth from them alternative ways of thinking and speaking. In so doing, the "bodily schema" of the subject shifted to the "operative language" of the flesh traversed by forces of "wild Being."

There are of course in this quest for an alternative "ontology of relatedness" many questions still calling for investigation. Some have to do with a clarification of Merleau-Ponty's own project. And most of these, as articulated earlier, draw attention to the flesh of the "field of Being," the nature of the forces which traverse it, the values implied by it, and the theology of its ontology. But the arena within this cluster of questions which most radically moves the truths of metaphysics into the field of historical relatedness is that of language and power.

If we were to register a lack in Merleau-Ponty's writings, it would be in respect to the operation of power as it is inscribed, sometimes brutally, in the bodies and flesh of the world today. Although Merleau-Ponty does give cursory attention to demystifying the power-relations of the "spectator," he fails to specify how these relations become embedded in the operations of language and carried within the cultural/linguistic frameworks of particular cultures. Thus, while the totalizing endeavors of political entities is critiqued by Merleau-Ponty, the totalizing effects of "dominant knowledges" as carried within a culture's linguistic habits is not. In order for a new "ontology of relatedness" to emerge, a more radical enterprise of demystification must take place—one that shows the complicity of power with knowledge and language, and exposes the inscription of abusive power upon the bodies of different cultural epochs. For such a project, we will turn in the next chapter to the cultural critique of Michel Foucault.

The last word though on Merleau-Ponty's philosophical quest ought to be his own. It is a word which needs to be kept in our own line of sight as we delve in the next chapter into multiple forms of the inscription of force upon bodies of the modern era. It is a word against all those who, either in the name of fixed absolutes or debilitating relativism, would close down the horizons of Being, immunizing themselves from its call. It is, in the end, a word of profound insight and hope.

These are the words which concluded the last article published by Merleau-Ponty prior to this death, the final lines of "Eye and Mind":

Is this the highest point of reason, to realize that the soil beneath our feet is shifting, to pompously name "interrogation" what is only a persistent state of stupor, to call "research" or "quest" what is only trudging in a circle, to call "Being" that which never fully "is"?

But this disappointment issues from that spurious fantasy which claims for itself a positivity capable of making up for its own emptiness. It is the regret of not being everything, and a rather groundless regret at that. For if we cannot establish a hierarchy of civilizations or speak of progress—neither in painting nor in anything else that matters—it is not because some fate holds us back; it is, rather, because the very first painting in some sense went to the farthest reach of the future. If no painting comes to be *the* painting, if no work is ever absolutely completed and done with, still each creation changes, alters, enlightens, deepens, confirms, exalts, re-creates, or creates in advance all the others. If creations are not a possession, it is not only that, like all things, they pass away; it is also that they have almost all their life still before them.[80]

Notes

1. Gianni Vattimo, "Metaphysics, Violence, Secularization," in *Recoding Metaphysics: The New Italian Philosophy*, ed. Giovanna Borradori (Evanston, Ill.: Northwestern University Press, 1988), 45.

2. Martin Heidegger, *Identity and Difference*, trans. Joan Stambaugh (New York: Harper and Row, 1969), 35–38. This interpretation of Heidegger is argued by Gianni Vattimo in "Toward an Ontology of Decline" in *Recoding Metaphysics: The New Italian Philosophy*, ed. Giovanna Borradori (Evanston, Ill.: Northwestern University Press, 1988), 63–75.

3. Maurice Merleau-Ponty, *Phenomenology of Perception*, trans. Colin Smith (New York: Routledge and Kegan Paul, 1962), xiii.

4. Ibid., xiii.

5. Due to the diversity of Merleau-Ponty's writings, they can be sorted in many ways. We are following the suggestion of Hugh Silverman that the seeds for Merleau-Ponty's thinking during his last two years can be found as early as 1955 in *Adventures of the Dialectic*, trans. Joseph Bien (Evanston, Ill.: Northwestern University Press, 1973). See Hugh J. Silverman, *Inscriptions: Between Phenomenology and Structuralism* (New York: Routledge and Kegan Paul, 1987), 130. Also see *Signs*, trans. R. C. McCleary (Evanston, Ill.: Northwestern University Press, 1964); "Eye and Mind," *The Primacy of Perception*, ed. James M. Edie (Evanston, Ill.: Northwestern University Press, 1964); and *The Visible and the Invisible*, ed. Claude Lefort, trans. Alphonso Lingis (Evanston, Ill.: Northwestern University Press, 1968).

6. Note that "empiricism" in this text refers both to the British philosophical empirical tradition and to its usage by the behavioral sciences in psychology. See Michael Hammond, Jane Howarth, and Russell Keat, *Understanding Phenomenology* (Cambridge, Mass.: Basil Blackwell Ltd., 1991), 146–7. Also, although Merleau-Ponty uses the term "intellectualism" throughout his work, we will use the more familiar term of philosophical idealism.

7. Merleau-Ponty, *Phenomenology*, 39.

8. Ibid., xiii.

9. See Silverman, *Inscriptions*, 63–91.

10. On p. 160 of *Signs*, Merleau-Ponty borrows Heidegger's term of the "unthought thought" to depict his own relationship to Husserl. The "unthought thought" is commonly recognized as a wealth of latent meaning, indwelling someone's work, but not fully articulated or exploited by the author her/himself. One could regard this as the "remainder" or "supplement" of a work which subverts the original authorial intention and yet, in doing so, calls for further reflection.

11. Terry Eagleton, *The Ideology of the Aesthetic* (Cambridge, Mass.: Basil Blackwell Inc., 1990), 7.

12. Note that the "pour-soi" and "en-soi" dichotomy of existentialist relations as set forth by Sartre and de Beauvoir are not accepted by Merleau-Ponty.

13. Merleau-Ponty, *Phenomenology*, 80.

14. Ibid., 80.

15. Ibid., 81.

16. Ibid., 81–2.

17. The example given by Merleau-Ponty is that of a person continuing to try to walk on a leg that has been amputated. The person "feels the missing limb in the same way as I feel keenly the existence of a friend who is not before my eyes," remaining "on the horizon" of one's life. See Ibid., 81.

18. Ibid., xiii.

19. On p. 62 of the *Phenomenology*, Merleau-Ponty says: "The mistake of reflective philosophies is to believe that the thinking subject can absorb into its thinking or appropriate without remainder the object of its thought, that our being can be brought down to our knowledge."

20. Ibid., 103–36.

21. The blind person's stick is an example used by Heidegger and Wittgenstein to illustrate the medium of tacit relations with the world. For Merleau-Ponty, the stick is part of the body's habits and such habits are "neither a form of knowledge nor an involuntary action." Ibid., 144. Akin to Heidegger's analysis of a tool as "ready-to-hand," the arm tends to withdraw from explicit attention as one concerns oneself with the work underway. One can see how this could lead to an analysis of fashion as body, a theme developed by "second-generation" feminists in *Fabrications: Costume and the Female Body*, eds. Jane Gaines and Charlotte Herzog (New York: Routledge, 1990).

22. Merleau-Ponty, *Phenomenology*, 93.

23. See Patrick Burke, "Listening at the Abyss," in *Ontology and Alterity in Merleau-Ponty*, eds. Galen A. Johnson and Michael B. Smith (Evanston, Ill.: Northwestern University Press, 1990), 81–97. Note that this differs from the abyss of

the Kantian sublime in that it is the abyss of the "in-between" of human relationships instead of one's relatedness to nature in general.

24. Merleau-Ponty, *Phenomenology*, 333.

25. Ibid., 325.

26. I agree here with M. C. Dillon who argues that Merleau-Ponty's "lived body" should not be equated with Kant's transcendental unity of apperception, and yet the "lived body" is "not free of the thesis of subjectivity." See pp. 17 and 25 of "Écart: Reply to Claude Lefort's "Flesh and Otherness," in *Ontology and Alterity in Merleau-Ponty*, 14–26.

27. On p. 211 of the *Phenomenology*, Merleau-Ponty claims that the origin of sensation is "a power which is born into, and simultaneously with (qui co-nait), a certain existential environment." Through a bodily "communion" (212) or "co-existence" (213) of subject and world, each is empowered to "be." This understanding of "connaisance" can be contrasted with the model of knowledge which Sartre attributes to realists and idealists, i.e., "to know is to eat, . . . we have all believed that the spidery mind trapped things in its web, covered them with a white spit and slowly swallowed them, reducing them to its own substance. What is a table, a rock, a house? A certain assemblage of 'contents of consciousness,' a class of such contents. O digestive philosophy!" See Jean-Paul Sartre, "Intentionality: a Fundamental Idea of Husserl's Phenomenology," trans. Joseph B. Fell, *Journal for the British Society for Phenomenology* 1, 2 (May 1970): 4–5, as quoted by Hammond, *Understanding Phenomenology*, 98.

28. Merleau-Ponty, *Phenomenology*, 430. Note that this "gap" not only maintains the irreducible "other," but is the "difference" which summons the self to expression, that is, to a self-transcending mode of subjectivity.

29. Ibid., 363.

30. Ibid., 363.

31. Ibid., 176.

32. Ibid., 177.

33. Ibid., 177.

34. Ibid., 182.

35. Ibid., 196.

36. Ibid., 197.

37. Ibid., 197.

38. Ibid., 194.

39. For this critique of Heidegger, see Charles E. Scott, *The Language of Difference* (Atlantic Highlands, N.J.: Humanities Press International, Inc., 1987).

40. Merleau-Ponty, *The Visible and the Invisible*, 200.

41. Ibid., 176.

42. Ibid., 48.

43. This critique is directed at the philosophy of his friend, Jean Paul Sartre, who is said to have "described our factual situation with more penetration than had ever been done before" and yet remains speculative in his distinction between the "for-itself" and "in-itself" and doctrine of "nothingness." See Ibid., 87.

44. Maurice Merleau-Ponty, "Eye and Mind," 181.

45. Merleau-Ponty, *The Visible and the Invisible*, 215. Note how the invisible is not the reverse of the visible, but is its "frame" or "limit."

46. Merleau-Ponty, "Eye and Mind," 182.

47. Ibid., 185.

48. Merleau-Ponty, *The Visible and the Invisible*, 139. Note how this concept of the elemental is developed by Edward Farley as the "elemental passions" of the self in *Good and Evil: Interpreting a Human Condition* (Minn., MN: Fortress Press, 1990), 97–114. Farley's treatment of such passions as interwoven desires for self-presencing, reciprocal relations, and meaning has resonances with both Merleau-Ponty's and Kristeva's notions of embodiment. One difference of emphasis though is in respect to the origins of the elemental. While Farley locates the origin in a "lack" of the self, Merleau-Ponty locates it in the plentitude of the "gap."

49. Merleau-Ponty, "Eye and Mind," 188.

50. Merleau-Ponty, *The Visible and the Invisible*, 76.

51. One is reminded here of the "madness" of knowing in Plato's *Phaedrus*. Note Merleau-Ponty's reference to the "madness of vision" in *The Visible and the Invisible*, 75.

52. This "phantom" for Merleau-Ponty is connected with the "fundamental narcissism of all vision" whereby one "is seen by the outside" of one's body and thereby "seduced, captivated, alienated by the phantom." Ibid., 139. This theme is elaborated upon further by Julia Kristeva in her discussion of "primary narcissism." See *Tales of Love*, trans. Leon S. Roudiez (New York: Columbia University Press, 1987).

53. Merleau-Ponty, "Eye and Mind," 188.

54. Merleau-Ponty, *The Visible and the Invisible*, 107.

55. Ibid., 211.

56. Ibid., 208.

57. For a fuller rendition of this, see my paper, "The Body Aesthetics of Wild Being," presented at the Rocky Mountain/ Great Plains Regional Meetings of the American Academy of Religion, May 1992.

58. Ibid., 201.

59. Ibid., 201.

60. Ibid., 88.

61. Ibid., 141.

62. Ibid., 141.

63. Ibid., 143. Note the contrast between this world which extends "beyond" the subject's experience and the world in the *Phenomenology* which had no existence unrelated to the "body/subject."

64. Ibid., 193.

65. This is argued by Galen A. Johnson in "Introduction: Alterity as a Reversibility," in *Ontology and Alterity in Merleau-Ponty*, xxii–xxxiv.

66. Ibid., 76.

67. Ibid., 144.

68. Ibid., 82.

69. Ibid., 200.

70. See Ibid., 153 where Merleau-Ponty suggests a shift from the "flesh of the world" to "language."

71. Ibid., 154. An example of the "speaking world" in "Eye and Mind" is on p. 273: "No more is it a question of speaking of space and light; the question is to make space and light, which are there, speak to us." Thus, the significations are already implicit in the world and call for the articulation of the artist.

72. Ibid., 126.

73. Ibid., 126. Note that this "openness" upon Being means that the past and future are no longer collapsed into the present, an important aspect of poststructuralist notions of time.

74. Ibid., 102.

75. Ibid., 153.

76. Ibid., 126. Note that such "offense" is part of the transgressive nature of language which is "un-authorized."

77. See above for the example of flesh as water in the pool being the place where the "visibles" materialize but are not contained. Also on p. 126 of *The Visible and the Invisible*, he says, "It is the error of the semantic philosophies to close up language as if it spoke only of itself." Note the similarity between this emphasis on language as flesh and Heidegger's portrayal of language as "the element" of multiple meanings akin to the waters within which a fish dwells. On p. 71 of *What is Called Thinking?*, he says: "The depths and expanses of its waters, the currents and quiet pools, warm and cold layers are the element of its multiple mobility. If the fish is deprived of the fullness of its element, it if is dragged on the dry sand, then it can only wriggle, twitch and die. Therefore, we always must seek out thinking, and its burden of thought, in the element of its multiple meanings, else everything will remain closed to us."

78. Ibid., 102.

79. Merleau-Ponty, "Eye and Mind," 163.

80. Merleau-Ponty, "Eye and Mind," 190.

CHAPTER THREE

Bound to the Back of a Tiger: Body as Site of Power/Knowledge Practices

> If I wanted to shake this tree with my hands, I should not be able to do it. But the wind, which we do not see, tortures and bends it in whatever direction it pleases. It is by invisible hands that we are bent and tortured most.
>
> —Friedrich Nietzsche, *Thus Spoke Zarathustra*

Introduction

Michel Foucault, a philosopher of European culture from the Enlightenment to the twentieth century, is fascinated by the interrelation of the "invisible" with the "visible" in the constitution of thinking and being. Like Nietzsche before him, Foucault aligns the "invisible" with shifting patterns of rationality that prevailed in the dominant practices of classical and modern Europe. Also like Nietzsche, he regards these rationalities primarily as constraints on the body, as the hands by which "we are bent and tortured most."[1] Thus, from his investigations of the history of madness to that of punishment to that of sexuality, he is intent on disclosing the mystifications of rationalities in their exclusionary mechanisms of power.

If Nietzsche's philosophical quest was compelled by the question, "Who is speaking?"—thereby drawing attention to covert operations of power in the positing of truth—Foucault's quest is drawn by a more contemporary version of that same question. Like other twentieth-century thinkers influenced by the nineteenth-century tradition of suspicion, Foucault also seeks to discern invisible dynamics of power, but shifts from a focus on the subject to that which speaks through the subject. For him, the question is: "What is language? What is a sign? What is unspoken in the world, in our gestures, in the whole enigmatic heraldry of our behavior, our dreams, our sicknesses—does all that speak, and if so in what language and in obedience to what grammer?"[2]

It is not the self-conscious subject but language that speaks. And Foucault, like other contemporary thinkers loosely gathered under the rubric of poststructuralism, is lured by the "vast play of language"[3] and invited to find a way "to make it appear in itself, in all its plentitude,"[4] to ask, "what language is in its being."[5]

So the "invisible" for Foucault, as he states in his introduction to *The Order of Things*, is not dependent upon the consciousness of a thinking subject—whether framed in the categories of Descartes, Kant or Husserl. Nor is it dependent upon some hidden internal structure of discourse, some "depth grammer" or internal code that orders the play of language and fixes its meaning. The question of the "being" of language for him is not a metaphysical quest—a search for a unifying structure of consciousness or language—but an investigation of the practices of a cultural epoch which give rise to varying modes of rationality and subjectivity.

In this shift of focus from the intentionality of a "transcendental consciousness" and from fixed structures of language to the dynamic interplay of discursive practices, Foucault betrays not only the influence of Nietzsche but that of Merleau-Ponty as well. As presented in the previous chapter, Merleau-Ponty in his later writings struggled with the metaphysical biases of phenomenology and structuralism, and ultimately moved toward an analysis of language as the "flesh" of the world traversed by "wild Being," a position later associated with poststructuralism. Foucault also seeks to interpret the dynamics of flesh, but explores with more rigor than Merleau-Ponty the power dynamics of this flesh in the material fields of the histories of madness, discipline, and sexuality. In such an analytics of power, he provides a more thoroughly historical and detailed understanding of flesh than provided by his predecessor.

But in exploring with such fervor the analytics of power within the play of language, Foucault seems to some readers to retreat into a new form of determinism—a collapse of all meaning to these dynamics, and thus a loss of the question of "being" as it pertains to an alternative vision of relatedness. Against this accusation, I contend that Foucault did not succumb to a nihilism of power dynamics but continued to be led by the question of the being of language. Yet in his pursuit of this question through the intricacies of the material practices of cultures, he was too suspicious of the contraints of stable truths on historical bodies to retreat into an alternative truth himself. Therefore, in pursuing the question of being, he allowed the question itself to shift, for being to become an enigmatic "aesthetics of existence" rather than a fixed "structure of existence," and for a new "ontology of relatedness" to be integral to this aesthetics.

In order to argue for and expand upon this interpretation of Foucault's work, especially as it pertains to the issue of "transgressive corporeality," we will in this chapter trace two developments in his thinking: one depicted as "archaeological" and presented in *The Order of Things*, and the other depicted as "geneaological" and presented in such works as *Discipline and Punish*, the *Power/Knowledge* essays, and *The History of Sexuality*. By following these two developments, I hope to show how Foucault's pursuit of the question of being in language tied to an "aesthetics of existence" is both in continuity with Merleau-Ponty's work on embodiment, including his struggle toward an alternative mode of vision and relationality, and goes beyond it.

The body for Foucault, as for Merleau-Ponty before him, is an arena of "wild Being," a site inscribed by technologies of power but not reduced to them. And for all those who would try to tame the body, to those who "believe ourselves bound to a finitude which belongs only to us, and which opens up the truth of the world to us by means of our cognition,"[6] Foucault gives a warning. We are not, he reminds us, as embodied beings, reducible to consciousness or to structures of language or to technologies of power. Instead, we are sites for the interplay of power/knowledges. And as sites for this interplay, including both the inscription of and resistance to dominant modes of power/knowledge, we cannot and will not be tamed. Instead of being bound to that "which belongs to us," we are, willingly or not, as embodied beings, "bound to the back of a tiger."[7]

An Archaeology of the Interplay of the "Invisible" and "Visible" in the Classical and Modern Eras

It is no accident that Foucault begins *The Order of Things* with an analysis of "Las Meninas" and ends with the metaphor of man as a "face drawn on sand at the edge of the sea." These images frame his analysis of the invisible within the visible during the classical and modern periods, including ways in which the invisible evokes certain modes of rationality which then, without explanation, disappear to make way for new ones.

In proposing that Foucault's analysis is moving toward an ethical sensibility, I am not suggesting that he is constructing a normative ethic, a position stipulating what people ought to do or how the world ought to be. Rather, by revealing the underlying regulatory practices of cultural epochs since the Enlightenment, he shows how these practices are linked to modes of self-constitution that tend to absorb nature and world in a self-reflexive gesture. The failure of the thinking subject to complete itself in this union of subject-object relations creates a space for a nonmetaphysical "ontology of relatedness," depicted by Foucault as an "aesthetics of existence." But what are these cultural epochs? What is the role of the invisible in the constitution of selves throughout these periods? And how does this archaeological enterprise open up a new space for thinking the body as an alternative to self-reflexive modes of human becoming?

"Las Meninas" is a painting by Velazquez which Foucault calls a representation of Classical representation,[8] an era beginning in Western culture around the middle of the seventeenth century. Prior to this time, particularly during the Renaissance but reaching as far back as the Stoics, the world was experienced as a ternary structure of text, signs, and similitudes. The text or invisible order of the world was revealed through signs that were connected by an unbroken chain of resemblance. Therefore, to "search for a meaning is to bring to light a resemblance. To search for a law governing signs is to discover the things that are alike."[9] The "prose of the world" was the world's revelation of its being within this universal field of resemblance.[10]

By the late sixteenth and early seventeenth centuries, the assumed linkage between signs and things had become problematic. "It is a frequent habit," says Descartes in his *Regulae*, "when we discover several resemblances between two things, to attribute to both equally, even on points in which they are in reality different . . ."[11] Not only for Descartes, but also within the wider practices of seventeenth-century culture, "resemblance" began losing its status as the vehicle for truth, and with this loss came a crisis of knowledge. If the kinship between signs and things (or between the signifier and the signified) could no longer be assumed, then what would assure access to the true meaning of things? How are we to discriminate, Enlightenment thinkers asked, between truth and illusion?

The answer offered in the writing of dominant theorists like Descartes and Bacon was a turn to the human intellect or thinking subject as the medium of true knowledge and thus of certainty. And their main goal was to rid the mind of the distortive influence of the senses so that the mind could discover within its own thought processes those representations that accurately depicted "reality-in-itself." Therefore, for the Classical Era, roughly designated by Foucault as 1650 to 1800, the thinking subject was the new locus of truth. Analytic thought replaced the "hierarchy of analogy." A finite enumeration of things or system of signs replaced the infinite interplay of Renaissance similitudes. "True and certain judgment" replaced the earlier probabilities of relations. And the human sciences became a separate enterprise from the natural sciences.[12]

All these features of "Classical rationality" were dependent on mind as an "absent" or nonparticipatory entity that ordered the world through the discrimination of objective identities. Like the absent sovereigns in "Las Meninas,"[13] the neutral spectator of Classical thought existed as an invisible locus of meaning, the source and foundation of true knowledge but not yet itself subject to scrutiny. "In Classical thought, the personage for whom the representation exists . . . he who ties together all the interlacing threads of the 'representation in the form of a picture or table'—he is never to be found in the table himself. Before the end of the eighteenth century, 'man' did not exist."[14]

In summary, in the shift from Renaissance to Classical (Enlightenment) rationality, the invisible chain of being revealed through resemblance was replaced with an invisible disembodied subject who represented the world to him/herself. The ternary structure of sign, signified, and similitude was replaced with the binary structure of mind/body and reason/feeling. And the sensual world, which in the Renaissance was valued for its hints of the sacred, was now shorn of its mystery and brought under the scalpel of reason.

But the reign of Classical representation with its insistence on a system of signs that would display the meaning of things had within it the seeds of its own demise. What it could not name without residue were the unruly powers of desire. And such desire "battering at the limits of representation" in the writing of Sade and others like him at the onset of the nineteenth century, posed a new problematic and prompted a shift into the Modern episteme.

What was this problematic? With the conditions for the truth of representation losing their self-evident status, cultural interrogation shifted to those powers or motivational forces which served as sources or origins of the representational structure of identities and differences.[15] And the sources or "transcendentals" which made objective knowledge possible in the modern era were "the force of labor, the energy of life, and the power of speech."[16] These together constituted the internal relations of organisms along with their temporal succession or external relations in history. Spatial values gave way to temporal ones. And the taxonomical gaze of Classical thought gave way to the observed/observer of humanism. The modern era is the scene for the emergence of "man."

In this shift from the Classical to Modern era, one of the most important areas of interest for Foucault is the change in modes of subjectivity. The invisible for the Classical era was the autonomous subject, with emphasis on the essence of the self as consciousness or mind. Body in this episteme was an extension of mind, a part of the empirical world and thereby open to the same taxonomical gaze as other parts of nature. The subject itself, depicted as disembodied mind, was a "given," an unexplored invisible not yet needing or inviting investigation.

In the shift to the Modern Era, the subject becomes a "strange empirico-transcendental doublet"—still representing the world to him/herself as an allegedly neutral metasubject of knowledge, but now, in addition, becoming knowledge's own proper object.

> Man appears in his ambiguous position as an object of knowledge and as subject that knows; enslaved sovereign, observed spectator, he appears in the place of the king, which was assigned to him in advance by "Las Meninas," but from which his real presence has for so long been excluded. As if, in that vacant space towards which Velezquez's whole painting was directed . . . all the figures whose alternation, reciprocal exclusion, interweaving, and fluttering one imagined . . . suddenly stopped their imperceptible dance, immobilized into one substantial figure, and demanded that the entire space of the representation should at last be related to one corporeal gaze.[17]

Representational thinking continues, but is now collapsed into the self-reflexive structure of Hegelian and post-Hegelian thought. "Man" becomes the invisible locus of all meaning and truth. And man's "other" becomes in a way different from the Classical period, "the Same as himself."[18]

Yet modern thought, in exploring the conditions of its own representations, soon discovers its limits as well.

> Man has not been able to describe himself as a configuration in the 'episteme' without thought at the same time discovering both in itself and outside itself, at its borders yet also in its very warp and woof, an element of darkness, an apparently inert density in which it is embedded, an unthought which it contains entirely, yet in which it is also caught.[19]

The "unthought," or that which disturbs and disrupts the Modern project of reflection, prevents "man" from forming a new positivity, and yet, in its displacement of the thinking subject, creates a space for thinking beyond metaphysics. It is in thinking the "limits" of "man," that is, in thinking those forces of the will-to-power which traverse the "warp and woof" of human existence, wherein a new mode of rationality and subject emerge.

In depicting our situation today as a threshold for "a space in which it is once more possible to think,"[20] Foucault appeals to Nietzsche's image of the "death of God" as linked to the "disappearance of man." Only in the demise of both invisibles do the fragments appear that solicit new thinking. Only in the dethroning of the sovereign—whether that sovereign be that of the pre-Classical God, the Classical "thinking subject," or Modern "man," will the future open to us with a new promise and task. It is at this threshold that Foucault ends his archaeology of the human sciences. For further clues to the nature of this new thinking, one must turn to his geneaologies of the material practices of Western culture within which all thinking comes into play. And the practices that called for further thinking by Foucault and now draw our attention, are those of discipline and sexuality. It is to the histories of these practices that we now turn.

A Geneaology of Discipline: the Soul as Prison of the Body

Two events occurred between the writing of *The Order of Things* and *Discipline and Punish* that shifted the motivation for and emphasis of Foucault's historical work. The first was the uprising of French students and workers in May, 1968. Whatever the complex of factors that caused these protests, they were a rude reminder to Foucault and other French intellectuals of the power dynamics just below the surface of their culture's institutions and knowledges. Although Foucault had in his earlier work criticized the truth claims of such knowledges or rationalities he now set out to show with greater zeal and precision the ways in which these claims grew out of and operated within the material practices of that culture.

In 1971, Foucault joined a small group of Parisian intellectuals in starting the "Groupe d'Information sur les Prisons" (GIP), a vehicle for prisoners to speak about prison conditions to the wider society. During this time, he began researching the history of penal theories and institutions, gave lectures on this topic at the College de France, and wrote his book, *Discipline and Punish*.[21] Thus, the writing of this book was motivated by more than a narrowly defined academic interest.

The second event which influenced Foucault at this time was the publication of several books by his friend, Gilles Deleuze. Deleuze's book on Nietzsche, published in 1967, presented Nietzsche's entire philosophy as an analysis of the "will-to-power." According to this analysis, all apparently solid and fixed entities—such as "facts," "man," and "reality"—are no longer to be understood as existing prior to interpretation or outside of a relational context. Deleuze uses the term "body" to depict the nature of humans as nodes for the crossing of relations of force. And in this shift of understanding from "selves" as fixed entities to "bodies" as entities shaped within a network of relations, Foucault follows suit.

Two other books by Deleuze, *Logigue du sens* and *Difference and Repetition*, extend this theme by shifting from a metaphysics of "facts" and "man" as fixed entities to a radically new mode of metaphysics. Foucault applauds this shift and speaks of it in terms of an understanding of the "event."

> To consider a pure event, it must first be given a metaphysical basis. But we must be agreed that it cannot be the metaphysics of substances, which can serve as a foundation for accidents; nor can it be a metaphysical coherence, which situtates these accidents in the entangled nexus of cause and effects. The event—a wound . . . is always an effect produced entirely by bodies colliding, mingling, or separating, but this effect is never of a corporeal nature . . . [it is] without thickness, mixture, or passion.[22]

Whatever this new metaphysics is for Foucault, it does not deal with substances and totalities (coherence) but with surfaces and difference. It deals with the continual displacement of the present and deferral of fixed meaning, "the [multiple] eternity of the [displaced] present."[23] It deals with the subject, not as a "synthesizing-synthesized entity," but as an "uncrossable fissure."[24] It tries to liberate difference "through the invention of an acategorical thought."[25] And it creates an ontology where "being is no longer a unity that guides and distributes [differences]," but rather is itself "the recurrence of difference."[26]

Propelled then by the events of May 1968 and by Deleuze's call for a new metaphysics, Foucault set his sights on one arena for an analysis of changing complexes of power/knowledge relations—that of the penal system and discourse. And the different sets of relations that he saw developing within Western Europe within the discontinuities of this discourse roughly followed the pattern of his earlier analysis. Again Foucault followed the paradigms of the Renaissance, Classical, and Modern Eras, but this time he drew upon detailed primary sources to depict the archaeology of each episteme, and extended his analysis to include a geneaology of the shifts from one episteme to another. If "soul" throughout this study of penal institutions is the "invisible" that establishes the network of interrelations of things without itself being open to scrutiny and evaluation, then "soul" is the "prison of the body," and Foucault's history of penal discourse and institutions is an archaeology and geneaology of the "soul."[27]

Like *The Order of Things*, *Discipline and Punish* has a frame that reveals the inner operations of the entire study. The book begins with a picture of two tortures, occurring several decades from each other. It ends with the "carceral city" of modernity. Between the beginning and the end, physical torture changes to psychological torment and physical dismemberment to corporeal fragmentation, but the ruthlessness of punishment is not necessarily mitigated. The brutal war of the king against those few who dared defy his power becomes in the Modern era "the ruthless war of all against all."[28] But in order to hear this argument in more detail and then ask what ramifications it might have for our study of "transgressive corporeality," we must first turn to the history of torture, punishment, and discipline in Europe as set forth by Foucault.

Discipline and Punish begins with a wrenching depiction of the torture and protracted suffering of a man who in the mid-eighteenth century tried to kill the king. Damien's crime was not so much a crime against the people as a threat to the power of the king, and therefore his punishment was not so much for the purpose of establishing justice as for the reactivation of a threatened power.[29] The truth of the sovereign had been called into question, and the body of the criminal had to bear the marks of the king's fury and strength.[30] It had to become in its horrible suffering the visible manifestation of an invisible, but controlling presence. In this way, in a manner obvious to all the king's subjects, this body would reinstate the "reign of truth" of that era.

But such a ruthless display of autocratic power had its limits. For in this "theatrical representation of pain," the imaginations of the people were provoked and their own violent passions stirred. Sometimes this worked to the advantage of the king. Whatever "technique of pain" was prepared for the hapless victim by the royal courts, the taunts and abuse of the mob could intensify its effects.

Yet once unleashed, such passions could break through the controls and sanctions of the sovereign to wreck havoc on his plans. Repelled by the unrestrained exercise of legal violence in public executions against one of their own, the common people often felt a kind of solidarity with the victim and with each other against the agents of power. And "it was this solidarity much more than sovereign power that was likely to emerge with redoubled strength."[31] Therefore, in failing to frighten the people into submission, the tortures not only failed to be a deterrent to crime but actually stimulated and provoked its spread.

The ineffectiveness of public executions to suppress crime along with the risk of counterviolence were factors in the largely unconscious shift to two other technologies of punishment that emerged within the eighteenth century and vied for dominence. The first, girded in the "technology of representation,"[32] was dependent on the new rationality and taxonomical gaze of the Classical Era. Foucault depicts this supposedly "gentle way of punishment" as integrally linked to the rise of social contract theory with its utilitarian ethic and rationality of representation.

Several features of the Classical "technology of power" are as follows:

1. That a rational link be established between the nature of the crime and its punishment. For example,

> those who abuse public liberty will be deprived of their own; those who abuse the benefits of law and the privileges of public office will be deprived of their civil rights; speculation and usury will be punished by fines; theft will be punished by confiscation; 'vainglory' by humiliation; murder by death; fire-raising by the stake.

> In the case of the poisoner, 'the executioner will present him with a goblet the contents of which will be thrown into his face; thus he will be made to feel the horror of his crime by being offered an image of it; he will then be thrown into a cauldron of boiling water.'[33]

Even though the severity of the punishment is not necessarily lessened, it now conforms to the logic of a social/political system rather than the whims of a king.

2. Because crime has weakened the "useful, virtuous" interests inherent in all humans, punishment must make the moral life more attractive. This reverses the earlier relations of morality and crime "so that the representation of the penalty and its disadvantages is more lively than that of the crime and its pleasures."[34]

3. Although society does have incorrigibles who must be eliminated, most criminals can be reformed. Thus, not only the nature of the punishment but its duration as well should be calculated to achieve the effect of a reformed and useful citizen.[35]

4. Because the crime is not against the king but against society, the punishment should be visible and useful to all. By putting criminals to work on chain gangs and other public works, they become the objects "of a collective and useful appropriation."[36]

5. All of this is designed to reinstate and strengthen the power of the law which represents the morality of the people.

> In physical torture, the example was based on terror: physical fear, collective horror, images that must be engraved on the memories of the spectators, like the brand on the cheek or shoulder of the condemned man. The example is now based on the lesson, the discourse, the decipherable sign, the representation of public morality. It is no longer the terrifying restoration of sovereignty that will sustain the ceremony of punishment, but the reactivation of the code, the collective reinforcements of the link between the idea of crime and the idea of punishment. In the penalty, rather than seeing the presence of the sovereign, one will read the laws themselves. The laws associated a particular crime with a particular punishment. As soon as the crime is committed, the punishment will follow at once, enact-

ing the discourse of the law and showing that the code, which links ideas, also links realities.[37]

6. And finally, as in Plato's *Republic*, there must be cooperation from the entire populace in the reencoding of virtuous behavior so that moral heros are praised instead of criminals. This of course is especially true of the poets.

> Instead of those songs of praise that turn the criminal into a hero, only those obstacle-signs that arrest the desire to commit the crime by the calculated fear of punishment will circulate in men's discourse . . . Discourse will become the vehicle of the law: the constant principle of universal recoding. The poets of the people will at last join those who call themselves the 'missionaries of eternal reason'; they will become moralists. "Filled with these terrible images and salutary ideas, each citizen will spread them through his family and there, by long accounts delivered with as much fervour as they are avidly listened to, his children gathered around him, will open up their young memories to receive, in imperishable lineaments, the notion of crime and punishment, the love of law and country, the respect and trust of the magistrature. Country people, too, will be witnesses of these examples and will sow them around their huts, the taste of virtue will take root in these coarse souls, while the evil-doer, dismayed at the public joy, fearful at the sight of so many enemies may abandon plans whose outcome will be as prompt as it is gloomy."[38]

In summary, through this carefully calculated structure of reform, punishment becomes a procedure evenly distributed throughout society for making people virtuous and law-abiding citizens. By "recodification of the mind," crime is rationally addressed, treated, and effectively subdued. The law becomes naturalized and rationalized in the discourse of everyday life, and the multiple "tiny theatres of punishment" distributed throughout society create a "punitive city" in which good behavior is linked to intelligence and proper thinking, that is, to "the submission of bodies through the control of ideas."[39]

What may be surprising in this scene is the paucity of prisons in the seventeenth and eighteenth centuries as a form of punishment. Although incarceration was used throughout the Classical Era, it didn't gain prominence until the early nineteenth century. Yet once firmly in place, it became almost the only mode of punishment outside of the death penalty. As expressed by a person of the early nineteenth century: "If I betrayed my country, I go to prison; if I have killed my father, I go to prison; every imaginable offence is punished in the same uniform way. One might as well see a physician who has the same remedy for all ills."[40] One can detect in this comment the frustration of a person well-trained in the representational justice of the Classical Era. And along with that person, we wonder what prompted this change. Was it a change in attitude, a sign of moral progress and enlightened thinking, or was it a much more subtle but powerful shift in the material practices of that culture which in turn gave rise to a different "technology of power"? Foucault supports the latter alternative, and "discipline" is the key to his argument.

Disciplines, says Foucault, are those micro-practices of a culture that operate as the underside of its noble ideals and conscious rationalities. In the Enlightenment, undergirding the rhetoric of human emancipation, was a structure of "moral technologies" conducive to a greater degree of social control than that of earlier societies. The whole structure of reform in that era rested on changed behavior, and changed behavior, in turn, rested on the installation of societal norms in the minds of the people. These disciplines, emerging initially in the rationalities of "representation" of the Classical Era, explode with a vengance in the nineteenth century as a natural counterpart to new economic, juridical-political, and scientific needs. For a depiction of this new "grip" on the body, Foucault recounts the modern history of the rise of capitalism, democracy, and psychology.

Economically, the growth of the disciplines at the time of Napoleon paralleled the rise of capitalism. And the reason for this was the need of the capitalist enterprise to achieve three goals, i.e., efficiency or cost-effectiveness, pervasiveness or control over all parts of the social body, and pliable workers or a "docile, useful" group of subjects.

Likewise, in the political arena, the egalitarian juridical framework of democratic forms of government relied on the operation of disciplinary mechanisms that instilled a system of rights on the minds of the populace, ironically through systems of "micro-power that are essentially non-egalitarian and asymmetrical."[41] The hierarchy of the workplace, says Foucault, is the underside of the "legal fiction of the work contract." The classification, specialization, and distribution of individuals in relation to one another in class structures is the underside of the universal norms of "man." The machinery of discipline acting as a "counter-law," that is, counter to the rhetoric of the law, "supports, reinforces, multiplies the asymmetry of power and undermines the limits that are traced around the law."[42]

And finally, in the discourses of the nineteenth century, the disciplines combined an increase of power with the formation of knowledge, culminating in techniques of examination and surveillance.

> At this point, the disciplines crossed the 'technological' threshold. First the hospital, then the school, then, later, the workshop were not simply 'reordered' by the disciplines; they became, thanks to them, apparatuses such that any mechanism of objectification could be used in them as an instrument of subjection, and any growth of power could give rise in them to possible branches of knowledge; it was this link, proper to the technological systems, that made possible within the disciplinary element the formation of clinical medicine, psychiatry, child psychology, educational psychology, the rationalization of labour. It is a double process, then: an epistemological 'thaw' through a refinement of power relations; a multiplication of the effects of power through the formation and accumulation of new forms of knowledge.[43]

The sciences of "man," particularly those related to psychology, went hand in hand with the propogation of the disciplines of self-control.

The most explicit image of this new technology of power arising in the nineteenth century is Bentham's model prison, the Panopticon. Reversing the principle of the dungeon, this modern prison has a central tower with a supervisor, a person invisible to the prisoners, and yet able to see all movements within each cell. Like an invisible, omniscient deity, the supervisor watches without being watched, and the objects of his gaze, unable to see him, soon internalize "the look." The external gaze becomes an internalized and self-regulating mechanism, now oblivious to the anonymous power who actually dwells in the tower, and rendering, through no visible display of authority, a docile subject/object.

Surveillance through a multiplicity of panoptical mechanisms becomes the mode through which individuals in modern society are measured, assessed, diagnosed, cured, and made useful for industry and commerce. And the penal system is only the most obvious site of this mode of power/knowledge which operates as well in the wider apparatuses of society. "Is it surprising," says Foucault,

> that the cellular prison, with its regular chronologies, forced labour, its authorities of surveillance and registration, its experts in normality, who continue and multiply the functions of the judge, should have become the modern instrument of penality? Is it surprising that prisons resemble factories, schools, barracks, hospitals, which all resemble prisons?[44]

We are no longer in this era within the preClassical spectacle of the theatre, nor the Classical taxonomical table of representations. We are now enclosed within the normalization techniques of the panopticon. The "body" is imprisoned in society's "soul."

What implications does this have for assessing contemporary modes of subjectivity and moving toward an alternative "ontology of relatedness"? Foucault, like Merleau-Ponty, is critical of forms of self-constitution that objectify "selves" and make them serve utilitarian goals. Also, like his phenomenological predecessor, Foucault moves toward a radically alternative mode of subjectivity that resists this modern structure of constraint and abuse. But in his analytics of power as complicit with knowledge in the imprisoning of the "body," he is less sanguine than Merleau-Ponty about the strength of the grip that these technologies hold on the body. For Foucault, the most insidious and therefore pervasively powerful mode of power/knowledge is the modern one with its mirco-practices of panopticism operating throughout society with the complicity of its victims. Certainly, this grip is loosened somewhat by naming these powers, thereby bringing their operations into the open. But this is tedious work, always done at the local level, and never completely finished. One must ask what motivates and sustains such resistance, and furthermore, what makes the alternatives better than those which went before? To assist us in exploring this further and attempting a tentative response, we turn to the last arena of power/knowledge that Foucault explored—that of the history of the discursive and nondiscursive practices of sexuality.

A Geneaology of Sexuality: From Relations of Pleasure to Care of the Self

If the "soul" is the prison of the "body" in *Discipline and Punish*, then sexuality as a "fragment of the soul" is the invisible limit of embodied existence in Foucault's last work, *The History of Sexuality*.[45] In focusing on the problematics of sex within different historical/cultural epochs, Foucault augments his earlier critique by two new emphases.

The first emphasis has to do with the nature of power as productive as well as restrictive of bodies. Already in the writing of *Discipline and Punish*, Foucault questions the adequacy of the juridical notion of power as purely negative and restrictive. In the multiple dispersions of force operating through the disciplines, power is tactical and strategic, that is, not so much restricting "natural vital forces" as producing particular ways of "being-in-the-world." It is this positive or productive aspect of power that Foucault had not identified as clearly in earlier works, and in these later writings, gives more focused attention.[46]

In respect to this new emphasis, Foucault vies against the theory of repression held by some psychoanalytic Marxists, including Herbert Marcuse. According to this Marxist theory, the natural, healthy forces of human sexuality have been repressed in the Modern era ever since the birth of capitalism and rise of the bourgeois order. The liberation of the "body" then, for them, entails the overthrow of these restrictive forces, especially the confinement of sexual intimacies to monogamous marriage.[47]

For Foucault, himself a critic of bourgeois orders including the economic order of capitalism, the problematic of sexuality is more complex than that depicted by the theory of repression. Embarking on an ambitious project of tracing the history of the discursive formations of sexuality throughout Western

culture, he begins by insisting on sexuality as a domain constituted by certain configurations of power/knowledge.

> Sexuality must not be thought of as a kind of natural
> given which power tries to hold in check, or as an
> obscure domain which knowledge tries gradually to
> uncover. It is the name that can be given to a historical
> construct: not a furtive reality that is difficult to grasp,
> but a great surface network in which the stimulation
> of bodies, the intensification of pleasures, the incite-
> ment to discourse, the formation of special knowledges,
> the strengthening of controls and resistences, are
> linked to one another, in accordance with a few major
> strategies of knowledge and power.[48]

In the Modern Era, sexuality became centered on four
strategic unities: a hysterization of women's bodies, a pedagog-
ization of sex, a socialization of procreative behavior, and a
psychiatrization of perverse pleasure.[49] Yet in order to reveal
the operation of power within these unities, especially as it
pertains to the formation of "selves," one must trace the shifting problematics of sex within earlier periods. In the second
and third volumes of *The History of Sexuality*, Foucault goes
as far back as the fourth century B.C.E. to "practices of the self"
in Classical Greece. Following this, he skips to the Hellenistic
Era of the Roman Empire to investigate a shifting of such
practices in Stoicism and early Christianity.

Before taking a closer look at these eras, the second emphasis of Foucault's later work also deserves a preliminary note.
Following the writing of *The Order of Things*, Foucault was
hailed throughout France as a cultural structuralist, a disciple
of Saussure's linguistic theory that depicted "man" as radically
shaped by the structural conditions of "his" linguistic context.
Even though Foucault rejected this label, his use of the word
"episteme" and depiction of epistemes as shaped by the discursive practices of a culture left him open to this type of packag-
ing. And perhaps most irritating to Foucault, it thereby left
him vulnerable to the criticism of cultural determinism.

By the time of his writing on sexuality, Foucault had
corrected this interpretation of his work through a change in
terminology and emphasis. Instead of using the more static
notion of "episteme," he changed to that of "apparatuses of
power," a term which highlights the internal multiplicity of

forces within the texture of culture. For Foucault, this multi-plicity always includes the possibility of resistance as well as submission.[50]

In addition to this change in terminology, Foucault also changed emphases by expanding his notion of the material practices of culture from that of discursive unities to nondis-cursive ones as well. By doing so, he wasn't retreating into a premodern or modernist enterprise of discovering realities behind the veil of language. Rather, he was expanding our understanding of language from that of words to the "speech" of other cultural signs, including the architecture of prisons and "tools" of examination in modern schools and hospitals.

In an interview recorded in the *Power/Knowledge* essays, Foucault speaks of this nondiscursive aspect of power as that of "institutions." An "episteme," he says, is "a specifically discursive apparatus, whereas the apparatus in its general form is both discursive and nondiscursive, its elements being much more heterogeneous."[51] Such nondiscursive elements are all those significations which function "in a society as a system of constraint and which isn't an utterance."[52] His best known example is the architectual plan of a military school. For those appropriating Foucault's analysis to a feminist critique, these "institutions" include anything from "table manners and toilet habits" to the standardized visual images of femininity circulated by twentieth-century media.[53]

Given these two shifts of emphasis, that is, the productive capacity of power and the inclusion of nondiscursive elements in the material practices of culture, Foucault proceeds to exa-mine the "will-to-truth"[54] that arises out of the problematics of sexuality and thus drives the mode of questioning for different eras in Western culture. In doing so, he is not attempting to assess ideas, behaviors, or even ideologies, but rather to investigate "the problematizations through which being offers itself to be, necessarily, thought—and the practices on the basis of which these problematizations are formed."[55]

Turning then to his analysis of the Classical Era of ancient Greece, it is surprising that the most intriguing problematics of sex in that era were formed neither around the relationship of men to women nor that of men to other mature males, but instead, around that of men to boys. The reason for this was lodged in the relative autonomy of both free men and boys in respect to the processes of self-constitution as well as the ambiguities of relationship that this autonomy elicited.

In the relation of free men to their wives, it was an unspoken given that their relationship was for the purpose of governing a household and engendering legitimate offspring. The wife was under the authority of her husband, and therefore didn't receive instructions on how to act as an independent ethical agent. Her role was both to assist her mate in managing the household and to bear healthy children. In turn, the husband's role in respect to his wife was to train her to do her job well and to assure her of her privileged status as the only bearer of his legitimate children. Within this hierarchical arrangement, there were failings and shortcomings, but none of the ambiguity and play of two independent partners posturing vis-à-vis each other outside the regulations of civic and domestic duties.

In the relation of mature free men to others of the same gender and status, proper behavior was defined by "philia" rather than "eros." And the major reason for discouraging an erotic relation between two free males was the problem of "passivity" for adult men. In sexual relations, only one role was honorable for men, that is, "the one that consisted in being active, in dominating, in penetrating, in asserting one's authority."[56] Although this role was conducive to the relations of a free male to his wife or to slaves, it posed a problem in respect to his sexual relations with other free men. Therefore, on the whole, intimacies between mature men were to be confined to friendships that excluded physical penetration. For Plato, Socrates' restraint in relation to Alcibiades was the model for all adult male relations.

But the relation between free men and boys was different from either of the above. First, it was an erotic relation, a physical intimacy that was not only widely accepted, but even expected. Second, it was problemetic in that the boys were in training to be citizens or leaders of the community. Thus, they were, like their older counterparts, active and free by nature. Yet in the sexual act, they played the role of a passive recipient of the older men's desire. How then could a boy's freedom be maintained and encouraged within a set of relations that placed him in a passive role? Put otherwise, how could one "make the object of pleasure into a subject who was in control of his own pleasures"?[57] This was the problematic of sex that captured the imagination of male theorists in Plato's day and called for thought. As such, it was the practice that was critical for the ethical formation of young males and yet could not easily be defined and thereby put to rest. The "fragment of the soul" that called for thought in Classical Greece was the sexual relation between free men and boys. This relation became the "aesthetics of existence" for that time and place.

The solution of this problem was not new regulations and restrictions, but the emergence of a stylistics that depicted the "open game" of the relation, including its "preferences, choices, freedom of movement, uncertain outcome."[58] In other more socially regulated relationships, the "voluntary modera-tion" of the man was based on his relation to himself. Yet in the erotics of two relatively independent subjects, the game was both more complicated and more intriguing. "It implied self-mastery on the part of the lover; it also implied an ability on the part of the beloved to establish a relation of dominion over himself; and lastly, it implied a relationship between their two moderations, expressed in their deliberate choice of one another."[59] The "aesthetics of existence" of Classical Greek culture was born out of the interplay of these bodies.

In skipping forward to the second century c.e., beginning with a rendition of Artemidorus' *Interpretation of Dreams*, Foucault continues to present analogies between the constitu-tion of a self in his sexual relations and his position in the wider arena of society as an ethical, social subject. For both, the penis began to signify a form of self-control necessary for this process of self-constitution.

> The penis thus appears at the intersection of all these games of mastery: self-mastery, since its de-mands are likely to enslave us if we allow ourselves to be coerced by it; superiority over sexual partners, since it is by means of the penis that the penetration is carried out; status and privileges, since it signifies the whole field of kinship and social activity.

Self-control for the early period of the first millenium meant self-possession and that in turn meant the reduction of those tensions that would disturb and decenter the self. The most threatening of such tensions was that of sexual activity.[60]

The result was what may at first glance appear to be "a pronounced severity, an increased austerity, stricter requirements" on human conduct in this period. But that was not, argues Foucault, due to an increase in institutional power over individual sensibilities. Instead, it was the continuation of a cultivation of the self that during this period took on new features.

One of these features had to do with a growing conviction of the weakness of the individual—his intrinsic frailty and thus need for protection from the ravages of outside forces and inside desires.[61] The cultivation of the self entailed an intense process of self-examination. "What one is, what one does, and what one is capable of doing" became the new focus of attention. The coveted goal was a self invulnerable to the onslaughts of want, fear, and desire. And the mode for achieving this was the apparatus of confession.[62]

Even pleasure had to conform to this new art of self-constitution through control. Sex was not seen as evil in itself, but as dangerous depending on the kind of pleasure that it evoked. Seneca is among others in this period who warned against the pleasure of *voluptas*, that is, a pleasure initiated from outside of oneself and posing possibilities of violence, loss of control and uncertainty. Over against this, he proposed the pleasure of *gaudium*,

> a state that is neither accompanied nor followed by any form of disturbance in the body or the mind. It is defined by the fact of not being caused by anything that is independent of ourselves and therefore escapes our control. It arises out of ourselves and within ourselves. It is characterized as well by the fact that it knows neither degree nor change, but is given as a "woven fabric," and once given no external event can rend it.[63]

Later on, even this notion of pleasure would be reduced to the pleasure of relieving oneself, so that sexual activity became like any other process of bodily relief. In some cases, such as that of Diogenes, the relief of sexual tension didn't even require the physical presence of another person.[64] The only pleasure that was appropriate then was that which rid oneself of irritation. All else, especially the pleasure which made one vulnerable to tension and disturbance, was counter to the process of "care of the self."

This mode of self-possession was particularly important for the shifting relations of a man to his wife, and this constitutes the second significant change of the Hellenistic Era from that of the Classical. Whereas earlier the "play" of a man's relation to a boy had been a spur to creative thinking and art of being, the problematic of this era shifted from that of men and boys to that of husbands and wives. In the Imperial Era, the love of boys continued but lost much of its "intensity, its seriousness, its vitality, if not its topicality."[65] In its place arose the problematics of the constitution of the self within the marital relation. And it is this problematic that would eventually be influential in defining the boundaries of legitimate and illegitimate modes of sexuality in Western culture for centuries to come.

This attention to the personal relation between a man and his wife did not emerge out of the same problematic as the earlier one between men and boys. One reason for this was that women still were not regarded as having the natural temperament and freedom of a man, and therefore, although females were increasingly enticing, they remained by and large the lesser members of a hierarchical relation. The conjugal relation then didn't have the tensions of a truly egalitarian relation. In addition, although sexuality during this time was not considered evil, it did pose a threat to the man's self-control, and given his tendency to succumb to desire, it became increasingly important for there to be clear regulations for the legitimate exercise of sexuality. The art of marriage then had a different stylistics than that of Classical homosexuality, and its "play" was confined by the following three stipulations.

The first was a "monopolistic" principle that stipulated that there would be no sexual relations outside of marriage. This not only assured the wife of being the sole bearer of the husband's children, it also established a "symmetry of rights" within sexual relations that were supposedly analogous to those of wider social relations. According to the Stoics of that period, if women were expected to limit sexual activity to their husbands (as had been the case in Western culture for a long time), then men were also expected to limit sexual activity to their wives. Although this mandate was frequently broken by the husband, it did succeed in establishing an economy of guilt and confession by reminding the transgressor of his inherent weakness. If he were truly in control of his "self," then he would be able to resist temptations outside of marriage.

Second, there was in the marital relation a dehedonization

of sexual intercourse, lessening the dangerous possibilities of that activity. Although this didn't entail the elimination of pleasure from that relation, it did call for its careful curtailment. The timing, frequency, and allowable emotion of the act was to conform to the dictates of moderation and self-control.

Third, there continued to be a principle of "procreative finalization" for marriage or, in other words, the production of offspring as the sole purpose of sexual intercourse. Although this had been a goal of the marital relation in earlier periods, it had not been regarded as the exclusive purpose of all sexuality. With this change came the legitimization of only those modes of sexuality that begat children. All other modes were not only superfluous, but perhaps as well "against nature."

In summary, due to the frailty of human nature and possibility that sexual activity would hinder the development of the self, sexuality came under closer scrutiny and confinement. The conjugal bond between a man and his wife became the focus of attention and site for careful release of sexual tensions and engendering of children. All other modes of sexuality, while still allowable, were deproblematized and devalorized as relations of imperfection and human weakness. And pleasure, finding its legitimate expression only within the conjugal relation, was controlled to fit the requirements for the constitution of a self-possessed subject.

The art of existence which comes to prominence during this period is one centered around the question of the "self-in-relation" rather than that of the relation itself. It is the self that poses the problematic—its degree of freedom, universal form, proper relations to others, and, above all, "the procedures by which it exerts control over itself."[66] The erotics within this "aesthetics of existence" revolved around the "care of the self," and the "other" was useful to the extent that she or he aided this process. In sum, the ethical core of the "aesthetics of existence" that came into being during the Hellenistic Era was that of the mastery of self and others by free men. All else was configured around this goal.[67]

On Body, Being, and the Ethical Relation

What then does this say about the meaning of body for Foucault, his commitment to the "being" of language, and the notion of ethics as an "aesthetics of existence" within alternative modes of self-constitution and relationality? In this final section, we will tie together some of these themes as they are developed in the three texts previously discussed and conclude by suggesting ways in which they contribute to the overarching theme of "transgressive corporeality."

At the onset of this chapter, we used Foucault's image of body as the "back of a tiger"—indicating its wildness, beauty, and terror. Foucault, in the three texts discussed here, speaks of "body" as the site for the traversing of forces, including those of rationalities, discipline, and sexuality. What became clear in his rather detailed depiction of the history of these forces in Western culture was that these forces are not natural or universal traits of human nature, but rather invisible unities of power/knowledge that are lodged within the dynamics of language. As discursive and non-discursive practices, they are configured differently within different historical periods. Therefore, they impact the process of self-constitution in quite distinct ways.

Operating upon and within bodies, these power/knowledge complexes set limits for the attitudes and behaviors of people in any particular era. And the reason that Foucault gives for investigating the histories of these complexes is to reveal the "hegemonies of truth" that they set up and activate. By showing these truths as both relative to a particular era and enhancing the social and political power of some people over others, Foucault reveals their "mask" of truth, and thus vulnerability to currents of resistance and change.[68]

In setting up his studies in this way, Foucault avoids the pitfalls of cultural determinism, the reduction of forms of subjectivity to causal effects and social influences. For him, a cultural episteme, or what later became a network of apparatuses of power, is heterogeneous and fluid—often dominated by particular forms of power/knowledge but not reduced to them. For Foucault, there is always resistance or the possibility of resistance within the flux of power/knowledge configurations. The system remains open.

This continual openness or residue of order that allows for changes is what Foucault refers to as the "recurrence of difference," a term that he associates with the "being" of language. Such "being" prevents the internal play of culture from becoming too stagnant or fixed. As such, it is a political/

historical version of Jacques Derrida's "eternal play of signs" unhooked from a "transcendental signified."

But there is another aspect of the "being" of language that also garners Foucault's attention, and that is its link to ethics or an "ontology of relationship." From *The Order of Things* through *Discipline and Punish* to *The History of Sexuality*, Foucault persistently reveals ways in which the self is constituted through self-reflexive means that deny the intrinsic worth and value of the "other" in processes of self-constitution.

In his first work, one sees this in the relation between the invisible gaze and the visible field of objects. Whether the invisible is a medieval sovereign, a disembodied mind, or an internalized supervisor, the visible revolves around that gaze and has value only as it conforms to "his" mechanisms of control. This becomes even more obvious in the operation of the "gaze" within the material practices of torture, punishment, and discipline. Although each era reflects different types of relationships between the invisible and visible, the controls of dominant power/knowledges continue to inscribe themselves on the bodies of that era. The only real change in the effects of power from the preClassical and Classical periods to the Modern one is that this inscription becomes more deeply etched in the body and therefore more insidious.

Again, in the history of sexuality, Foucault shows the apparatuses of power by which different sexual relations are produced and constrained. One is impressed with the subtle ways in which bodily relations become circumscribed by the needs of a self in "his" constitution. It is evident in this account that not all people have access to such self-constitution. Even more problematic, the very processes by which the self is "cared for" are detrimental to healthy, human relatedness.

So even though Foucault could not, in faithfulness to his method, set up a final truth of relationship, he could and did show the limitations and constrictions of these other modes, and in so doing, called for something else. What remains troubling about his work is not so much his failure to provide new foundations for relationality as his reticence to give indicators about what an alternative mode of relationality might be like.

There is only one place in which he does this. In an uncharacteristic comment, Foucault, at the end of his first volume on *The History of Sexuality*, appeals to "bodies and pleasures" as the "rallying point for the counterattack against the deployment of sexuality" and thereby an arena for the emergence of a new ethical praxis.[69] But what in this text do "bodies and pleasures" mean?

Given the method of his critique throughout each of the writings cited above, we might assume that "bodies and plea- sures" refers to a stylistics of bodily relations which resist various forms of bodily constraint and thereby retain the "open play" of human interaction. Along with this, these terms might suggest a valorization of the pleasure of *voluptas*—that plea- sure which resists mechanisms of self-possession and self- protection by entering into the danger and wounding of nonde- fensive encounters with the "other." Perhaps they even suggest that the "eternal recurrence" or "being" of language can pro- vide clues for these modes of resistance and alternative ethical aesthetics.

But all this remains speculation, because Foucault, although expressing an interest in ethics throughout his life- time, refused to give definition to what might constitute healthy, human relatedness. In part, his reticence can be attributed to a respect for "local" critique and reconstruction. For him, the universal intellectual was passé, if not dangerous in his/her failure to recognize epistemological limitations. Therefore, the "tyranny of globalizing discourses" in general made him cautious about setting forth ethical mandates for all people in all places for all time.[70] This would have violated an important feature of his method.

And yet, one is left dissatisfied with the almost total lack of ethical direction in Foucault's writings. Given the urgency of our ethical crises today in respect to such things as nuclear war, economic exploitation, hunger, illness, and racial gene- cide, would it not be possible for one to resist the lure of a totalizing discourse and yet provide resources and guidelines for ethical thinking? Furthermore, could not the "being" of language with its internal play and possibilities of relationality be explored further as a resource for such thinking? In sum, must we stop at the threshold of the critique of destructive modes of human relationality, or is it possible to "transgress" these limits by garnering glimpses in word and deed of some- thing better? We are indebted to Michel Foucault for provoking such questions. We are obligated as participants in the global community threatened by horrendous forces of diminishment and destruction to go beyond his critique in the formulation of some answers, however incomplete and tentative they may be.

Notes

1. On p. 25 of *Discipline and Punish: The Birth of the Prison* (New York: Vintage Books, 1979), Foucault calls the body the site of power relations which "have an immediate hold upon it; they invest it, mark it, train it, torture it, force it to carry out tasks, to perform ceremonies, to emit signs."

2. Michel Foucault, *The Order of Things: An Archaeology of the Human Sciences* (New York: Vintage Books, 1973), 306.

3. Ibid., 307.

4. Ibid., 306.

5. Ibid., 382. Note that Foucault distinguishes between an interrogation of "the shining but crude being of language" and the Enlightenment theory of language as representation. See *The Order of Things*, 339.

6. Ibid., 322.

7. Ibid., 322.

8. Ibid., 16.

9. Ibid., 29.

10. *The Prose of the World* is a work which Merleau-Ponty began writing in the early fifties and never completed. If it is the precursor text to *The Visible and the Invisible*, as Claude Lefort has argued, then it is interesting that Foucault uses this phrase to depict the rationality of the Renaissance. By doing this, he may be suggesting that Merleau-Ponty in his later work was trying to retrieve a bond between the signifier and the signified that was neither natural nor merely conventional. See Maurice Merleau-Ponty, *The Prose of the World*, trans. John O'Neill, ed. Claude Lefort (Evanston, Ill.: Northwestern University Press, 1973), xix–xxi.

11. Foucault, *The Order of Things*, 51.

12. Ibid., 54.

13. On p. 13 of *The Order of Things*, Foucault speaks of the gaze of the two sovereigns as "completely inaccessible, because it is exterior to the picture, yet is prescribed by all the lines of its compositions."

14. Ibid., 308.

15. Ibid., 243.

16. Ibid., 244.

17. Ibid., 312 and 318.

18. Ibid., 328.

19. Ibid., 326.

20. Ibid., 342.

21. Eve Tavor Bannet, *Structuralism and the Logic of Dissent* (Chicago: University of Illinois Press, 1989), 129–33.

22. Michel Foucault, "Theatrum Philosophicum," in *Language, Counter-Memory, Practice*, trans. Donald F. Bouchard and Sherry Simon, ed. Donald F. Bouchard (New York: Cornell University Press, 1977), 173.

23. Ibid., 175.

24. Ibid., 179.

25. Ibid., 186.

26. Ibid., 187.

27. Michel Foucault, *Discipline and Punish: The Birth of the Prison*, trans. Alan Sheriden (New York: Vintage Books, 1979), 30.

28. Ibid., 307.

29. Ibid., 35.

30. Ibid., 55.

31. Ibid., 63.

32. Ibid., 104.

33. Ibid., 105.

34. Ibid., 106.

35. Ibid., 107–8.

36. Ibid., 109.

37. Ibid., 109–10.

38. Ibid., 112–13.

39. Ibid., 102.

40. Ibid., 117.

41. Ibid., 222.

42. Ibid., 223.

43. Ibid., 224.

44. Ibid., 227–8.

45. Michel Foucault, *The History of Sexuality*, Vol. 1: *An Introduction*; Vol. 2: *The Use of Pleasure*; Vol. 3: *The Care of the Self* (New York: Vintage Books, 1990).

46. Foucault, *Power/Knowledge Essays*, 184.

47. Herbert Marcuse, *Eros and Civilization: A Philosophical Inquiry Into Freud* (Boston: Beacon Press, 1966).

48. Foucault, *The History of Sexuality*, Vol. I, 105.

49. Ibid., 103.

50. Bennet, *Structuralism and the Logic of Dissent*, 169.

51. Foucault, *Power/Knowledge*, 197.

52. Ibid., 197–8.

53. Susan R. Bordo and Alison M. Jagger, eds., *Gender/ Body/Knowledge: Feminist Reconstructions of Being and Knowing* (New Brunswick, N. J.: Rutgers University Press, 1989), 13.

54. The French title of Foucault's first volume in *The History of Sexuality* is *La Volonte de savoir* or "the will to true knowledge." This indicates an affinity with Nietzsche's critique of a "will-to-truth" that privileges part of society by fixing the essense of a person or thing. See p. 79.

55. Foucault, *The Use of Pleasure*, 11.

56. Ibid., 215.

57. Ibid., 225.

58. Ibid., 202.

59. Ibid., 203.

60. Foucault, *The Care of the Self*, 34.

61. Ibid., 67.

62. Ibid., 68.

63. Ibid., 66.

64. Ibid., 139.

65. Ibid., 189.

66. Ibid., 238.

67. Ibid., 95.

68. Michel Foucault, "Truth and Power," *Power/Knowledge Essays*, 133.

69. Foucault, *The History of Sexuality*, Vol. I, 157.

70. Foucault, *Power/Knowledge Essays*, 83.

CHAPTER FOUR

On the Threshold of Madness: Speaking and Writing the Mother's Body

> He attempts to compose a discourse which is not uttered in the name of the Law and/or of Violence: whose instance might be neither political nor religious nor scientific; which might be in a sense the remainder and the supplement of all such utterances. What shall we call such discourse? erotic, no doubt, for it has to do with pleasure; or even perhaps aesthetic, if we foresee subjecting this old category to a gradual torsion which will alienate it from its regressive, idealist background and bring it closer to the body, to the drift.
>
> —Roland Barthes, *Roland Barthes by Roland Barthes*

Introduction

Although the invisible substratum of human becoming is understood differently by Merleau-Ponty and Foucault, for neither of them is this a static or peaceful realm. For Merleau-Ponty, the invisible is a field of relatedness traversed by the forces of "wild Being." Such Being, experienced by painters in their "bodily vision" of the world and by all humans in the "conaissance" of mutually enhancing relations, is not destructive, and yet operates through processes of decentering and depresentation. Thus, the body/self attains its unity, not through the operation of some fixed essence, whether human or divine, but through the "correlative encroachment" of corporeal interaction. Such a self is a "unity of transgression," and such an invisible is a dynamic field of transgressive relations.

Foucault both expands upon and intensifies the operations of the invisible by making it an historical realm, that is, traversed by the changing rationalities and power dynamics of Western culture. While Merleau-Ponty depicts the invisible largely in terms of plentitude and creativity, Foucault emphasizes its more sinister attributes. From the power of the sovereign in seventeenth-century Europe to the dispersed powers of disciplines internalized in "man" in more recent decades, the invisible is the site for the interplay of power/knowledges, a site around which meaning accrues, but only through the dynamics of domination and resistance. The self for Foucault is a body forged through the clash of competing power/knowledges, and a transgression of dominant power/knowledges for him, has a greater intensity and magnitude than that envisioned by his phenomenological predecessor. If the elemental fire of the field of Being for Merleau-Ponty ignites the creative imagination of the artist, for Foucault, it is the consuming flames of the apocalypse, reducing old epistemic structures to ashes in the cataclysmic creation of a new heaven and a new earth.

Julia Kristeva, a literary critic and psychoanalyst of French poststructuralism, also begins her depiction of the process of human self-constitution with an exploration of the invisible substratum of unruly relations. Like Foucault, she views this substratum as a place of assault on the self—not only an assault from without but also from within operating through the mechanisms of anguish and horror. Thus, the "empirical-transcendental doublet" of modern subjectivity is for her a body of "anesthetized wounds," trapped in melancholy and depression.[1]

While Foucault, by naming the apparatuses of power/knowledge that inscribe the body, invites resistance, Kristeva actually explores the processes by which a subject does resist.

Thus, like Merleau-Ponty, she pushes through the barriers of constraint to an alternative mode of subjectivity, a "split subject"—one that struggles against the anesthesia of technological society through the practice of "speaking." For Kristeva, that which poses the problematic of modern experience and thereby calls for articulation is an art of selfhood whose wounds are neither anesthetized nor cured, but are the source of new possibilities, not through an avoidance of pain but into its darkest recesses.

To follow Kristeva's analytics of subjectivity is to embark upon an erratic path winding its way through several centuries and disciplines. The temporal scope of her explorations ranges from ancient Greece to twentieth-century Europe. The academic breadth includes linguistics, psychoanalysis, literary criticism, philosophy, and the study of Judaism and Christianity. This chapter will focus on two stages in her work, the period prior to 1980 when she wove her analysis of language together with psychoanalytic theory, and the period following 1980 when these interests were expanded upon within the wider study of culture, literature, ethics, and religion.

In her dissertation, published in 1974, Kristeva first presents the thesis that the context of the "speaking subject" is language, and then proceeds to investigate the nature of this context. Language, she argues, is not tied to a fixed Archimedean point or "transcendental signified," but is instead a neverending dynamic interplay of three movements: the semiotic, symbolic, and thetic. Her analysis of this interplay connects these linguistic categories not only to psychoanalytic theory but also to those "signifying practices" which aid or thwart the emergence and functioning of the subject. Over against the practices of narrative, metalanguage, and contemplation, Kristeva sets forth "poetic language" as the most efficacious for processes of healthy human self-constitution. She brings her argument to a close in this early work by giving examples of poetic language in the writings of two nineteenth-century men.

Although Kristeva's early books, including *Revolution in Poetic Language* and *Desire in Language*, refer to a "third term," that is, the "thetic," as a border or lining of the "speaking subject," it isn't until 1980 that she gives more concerted attention to this border in her development of the notion of abjection. In *Powers of Horror*, a study with analogies to

Foucault's work, Kristeva presents a history of abjection, beginning with the ancient Greeks, continuing through the rituals and texts of ancient Judaism and Christianity, and ending with contemporary poetic literature. In this history, the abject is a mode of catharsis modulating the effects of "thanatos" and "eros" in the signifying practices of Western culture. We will follow these changes of abjection through Kristeva's later work in a section titled, "Abjection, the Mother's Body, and the Limits of Language."

In the final section, we will relate the dynamics of the "speaking subject" to ethics and religion. As suggested in various ways throughout her writing, Kristeva's alternative notion of subjectivity is neither girded in the firm foundations of essentialism nor teeters in angst on the brink of the abyss, but is rather a "subject in process/on trial" who persists in "dancing on a volcano."[2] The final section of this chapter will delineate the multifarious steps of such a dance.

The Ternary Dispositions of a "Speaking Subject"

Over against those British and American empiricists who view language as a tool for naming and communication, as well as French structuralists who view it as a monolithic, homogeneous structure embedded within human subjects and relations, Kristeva argues in her dissertation (one third of which is translated as *Revolution in Poetic Language*) for language as a heterogeneous process within which the "speaking subject" is constituted. Thus, the invisible substratum of human becoming for her is neither the transcendental/Cartesian ego nor language as a fixed structure but language as a complex and ever changing "signifying process."[3]

This process for Kristeva, following upon the analysis of both Freud and Lacan, has a ternary quality—three dispositions or energies interwoven with each other in the formation of a subject. The first, logically and developmentally prior to the others, is the semiotic. Based upon the Greek term "semeion," meaning "sign," the semiotic is a complex of sexual and emotive impulses traversing a child's body before the onset of identity. The place of such drives is the "chora," a word borrowed from Plato's *Timaeus* and used by Kristeva for: "a receptacle, unnameable, improbable, hybrid, anterior to naming, to the One, to the father, and consequently, maternally connoted."[4]

One of the earliest expressions of the impulses of the "chora" in the life of the child is laughter:

> Oral eroticism, the smile at the mother, and the first vocalisations are contemporaneous . . . During this period of indistinction between 'same' and 'other,' infant and mother, while no space has yet been delineated, the semiotic chora . . . relieves and produces laughter . . . The chora is indeed a strange 'space:' the rapidity and violence of the facilitations are localized at a point that absorbs them and they return to the invoking body without signifying it as separate; they stop there—impart the jolt—laughter.[5]

Thus, the chora is a site of "jouissance," literally, at least in this case, a "joy without words."

But even though the semiotic prevails developmentally in the pre-Oedipal stages of a child's life, it isn't limited to that, but returns in the post-Oedipal period as a disruptive force, an inbreaking of bodily impulses through laughter, music, and rhythm. These impulses can be channeled into powerful modes of ecstasy—some of which are destructive, as in psychosis and fascism, and some of which are positive and creative, as in religious mysticism and certain modes of art. One is a "madness" of cathartic violence; the other is a "holy madness" of nonviolent catharsis.[6] Much of Kristeva's writing focuses on the eruption of the semiotic into the institutions and practices of human life, and the problematic of its flow into one form of madness or the other.

The final two dispositions of the signifying process emerge with the onset of identity and continue in various modes throughout the life of the subject. The one given attention in Kristeva's early work is the symbolic—the impulse of order and representation located in the domain of propositions and shaping the sexual, linguistic, and social/political identities of subjects. Sexually, the symbolic establishes the binary identities of male or female, heterosexual or homosexual. Linguistically, it establishes the structures of grammar, syntax, and logic. And socially, it establishes the hierarchical structures of the nuclear family, capitalism, institutional forms of religion, and the State. Paternally connoted, the symbolic reflects Kristeva's adoption of Lacan's "Law of the Father," that is, that complex of social mechanisms through which the semiotic is harnessed, regulated, and used for purposes of personal and social stability.[7]

The symbolic then for Kristeva is a violent force. Far from being a tame, humanizing impulse, it operates out of fear and coercion, maintaining the unity and certainty of its structure by controlling the semiotic and asserting its mastery in times of crisis through the catharsis of sacrifice. Thus, it is a form of Nietzsche's "will-to-truth," a force that imposes a monolithic, homogeneous structure on a polymorphous and heterogeneous body. Like Nietzsche, Kristeva attempts to speak that which disturbs and disrupts the symbolic without either positing a better, truer one or collapsing all form into the amorphous, pre-Oedipal zone of undifferentiated semiotic impulses. Instead, her therapy is "aesthetic," moving toward a creative tension between the semiotic and symbolic in an "open structure" personality.[8] But to address the problematic of such an aesthetic, one must give attention to the border or threshold between these competing dispositions. Kristeva begins her exploration of this limit through the positing of the third term of the signifying process, that of the thetic.

The thetic, first enacted in the primary narcissism of a child's emerging identity, is reenacted as a continuing tension between the prohibitions of the symbolic and the disruptions of the semiotic. Kristeva defines the thetic in terms of the mirror stage and castration. The first of these, the mirror stage, is the entrance into language and thereby identity through a break with the mother's body, and differentiation of the subject from objects. This is accompanied by the discovery of castration, a lack which evokes desire, continually drawing the subject back to its impossible unity. The identity that is first produced then is only accomplished through a rupture of the thetic, a unification of the symbolic which is forever split, and the unceasing desire for overcoming this split. In order for the identity of such a "split subject" to be stable and yet open to the "other," the thetic must remain a permeable membrane, a "transversable boundary," a place of alterity through the "metonymy of desire."[9]

But the thetic, under pressure from the symbolic, can become rigid and resistant to the impulses of the semiotic, as it is prone to do in institutions and ideologies of technological society. A disruption of the thetic then entails a transgressive force—one that doesn't simply reform but dismantles the logic of the reigning symbolic order.

The problem, then, was one of finding practices of expenditure capable of confronting the machine, colonial expansion, banks, science, Parliament—those positions of mastery that conceal their violence and pretend to be mere neutral legality. Recovering the subject's vehemence required a descent into the most archaic stage of his positing, one contemporaneous with the positing of social order; it required a descent into the structural positing of the thetic in language so that violence, surging up through the phonetic, syntactic, and logical orders, could reach the symbolic order and the technocratic ideologies that had been built over this violence to ignore or repress it.[10]

So the thetic arbitrates between two forms of violence—the repressive violence of a symbolic order that hides under the mask of neutrality and truth, and the surging nonrational violence of the semiotic chora resisting the confinement of all form and order. If, as Rene Girard asserts, "only violence can put an end to violence,"[11] then the thetic too must be a violent force, counteracting the mutual destructiveness of the other dispositions. And the form of the thetic that Girard traces through the history of several religious traditions is that of sacrifice, the killing of a surrogate victim in order to relieve the body politic of psychic/social tensions, breaking the vicious cycle of "reciprocal violence," and thereby restoring social harmony.[12]

Although Kristeva too recognizes the function of the thetic as cathartic, modulating tensions between the symbolic and semiotic through a bolt of excess energy, she struggles with the hypothesis that this necessarily entails a violent, destructive response. In later works, through development of the idea of abjection and then of love, she sets forth alternative modes of catharsis operating throughout the history of Western culture—some destructive and some not. In these early writings, however, she sets the stage for later investigations by discriminating between two types of catharsis operating within the thetic.

The first form of catharsis, usually expressed in the rituals of religion, is that of sacrifice. Like Girard and Freud before him, Kristeva links this to "parricide at the origin of the social contract" operative in all societies. In response to the originating violence of parricide, a "sacred murder" is enacted, thereby attempting to confine violence to the sacrificial act and reestablish social order. "Sacrifice represents the thetic only as the *exclusion* establishing social order, *positing* the violence that was caught and lodged within murder as within an inaugural break. This positing—'a boundary to the infinite' [Mellarme]—is the basis on which socio-symbolic sets are structured."[13]

But sacrifice is not the only or perhaps the best means for subduing tensions engendered by the vicious struggle of the semiotic and symbolic. The other means is not related to parricide, the "origin" emphasized by Freud, but to incest, i.e., reunification with the "mother's body." This second cathartic practice, that of art, inundates the symbolic order through "dancing, singing, and poetic animality," and thereby provides a nonviolent means for the "flow of jouissance into language."[14] Art, then, while sometimes accompanying the practice of sacrifice, can also pose as its nonviolent alternative—one that not only redeems social harmony but does so with positive transformative effects.

> Whereas sacrifice assigns jouissance its productive limit in the social and symbolic order, art specifies the means—the only means—that jouissance harbors for infiltrating that order. In cracking the socio-symbolic order, splitting it open, changing vocabulary, syntax, the word itself, and releasing from beneath them the drives borne by vocalic or kinetic differences, jouissance works its way into the social and symbolic. In contrast to sacrifice, poetry shows us that language lends itself to the penetration of the socio-symbolic by jouissance, and that the thetic does not necessarily imply theological sacrifice.[15]

It is art then, and especially poetic language, and not sacrifice which is the means for the subversion and transformation of the social/symbolic unit—whether that of an individual or of a group.

In this shift from discussion of the ternary quality of the

signifying practices of a "speaking subject" to advocacy for poetic language, Kristeva, following a line of thought already set forth by Roland Barthes, seeks a "transgressive discourse" that is "not uttered in the name of the Law and/or of Violence," but is erotic, aesthetic, and close to the body. For Kristeva, poetic language can be transgressive because it is neither outside of the reigning social/symbolic order nor inside it, but at its limit. "To penetrate the era, poetry had to disturb the logic that dominated the social order and do so through that logic itself, by assuming and unraveling its position, its syntheses, and hence the ideologies it controls."[16]

Poetry accomplishes this dismantling of "truth" through the polyvalence and multidetermining nature of the word, a quality which Kristeva depicts as adhering to the logic of carnival. Drawing upon the work of Mikhail Bakhtin, she defines the "dialogism" of carnival as:

> the logic of distance and relationship between the different units of a sentence or narrative structure, indicating a becoming—in opposition to the level of continuity and substance, both of which obey the logic of being and are thus monological. Secondly, it is a logic of analogy and nonexclusive opposition, opposed to monological levels of causality and identifying determination. Finally, it is a logic of the "transfinite," . . . a poetic sequence (which) is a "next-larger" [not causally deduced] to all preceeding sequences of the Aristotelian chain [scientific, monological, or narrative].[17]

Therefore, through the polyvalence of the word, particularly that of poetry and fiction, the "identity, substance, causality, and definition" of the symbolic is transgressed so that an alternative logic may appear, one of the relations of becoming, of analogy, and of the transfinite.[18] For Kristeva, this alternative logic is put into effect through the writings of those on the fringe of official culture, that is, by writers such as Mellarme and Lautreamont in the nineteenth century and Baudelaire, Kafka, Bataille, and Joyce in the twentieth. In her early work, she gives primary attention to the former.

Kristeva's elaboration of the dynamic of poetic language includes two features which lead to new emphases in her later work. The first is a word of caution, admitting that poetic language—even that with transgressive force—can be co-opted by the symbolic order as a fetish and thereby rendered ineffective for personal or social change. Whenever the text becomes either a guardian of accepted meaning or, at the other extreme, falls into an "unspeakable delirium," it ceases to maintain "the difficult crossroad of heterogeneous contradiction with and in the symbolic order," and thereby fails to transform it. Neither "relaxation" nor "excessive attention" retains the play of the text, and it is in the play where the breakthrough of creative change occurs.[19]

The issue with which she closes her study is that of the relation of poetic language to ethics. As expected, in her survey of options in contemporary ethical theory, Kristeva rejects formalism, moralistic idealism, and vulgar sociologism—opting instead for ethics as a dimension of the signifying practice.

> "Ethics" should be understood here to mean the negativizing of narcissism within a *practice*; in other words, a practice is ethical when it dissolves those narcissistic fixations [ones that are narrowly confined to the subject] to which the signifying process succumbs in its socio-symbolic realization. Practice, such as we have defined it, positing and dissolving meaning and the unity of the subject, therefore encompasses the ethical . . . By stating scientific truths about the process of the subject [his discourse, his sexuality] and the tendencies of current historical processes, the text fulfills its ethical function only when it pluralizes, pulverizes, "musicates" these truths, which is to say, on the condition that it develop them to the point of laughter.[20]

The ethical then is that discourse or dimension of discourse that disturbs and disrupts the truths of a self, especially those truths rooted in narcissistic fixation. In doing so, it opens the self to that which posits, threatens, and transforms it. Never able to be fully stated or represented, the ethical for Kristeva can only be known as it is practiced. And poetic language "is one of the most accomplished examples of such a practice."[21]

Abjection, the Mother's Body, and the Limits of Language

If the thetic is Kristeva's depiction of the aesthetic limit of the "speaking subject" revitalized through poetic language, then the abject is the limit of the "speaking, loving subject" experiencing rebirth through wounds of relatedness. But in order to conceptualize the radical nature of this subject and then delineate its ramifications in terms of ethics and the sacred, one must follow Kristeva's meanderings through this notion of abjection in respect to the Oedipal Complex, the history of Judaism and Christianity, the dangers and potentials of cathartic practices, and the Mother's Body as dialogical limit. Along this journey, we will see the continuities of Kristeva's thinking as she persists in probing the ternary dispositions of human becoming, but we will also see those places where her analysis undergoes changes as she struggles with the multifaceted dynamics of a healthy subjectivity within the context of twentieth-century Western culture.

We begin, as Kristeva does, with the notion of abjection as an uncertain, ambiguous border of the corporeal self, a border which is a necessary condition of the subject and yet which in its negativity continually threatens the subject's integrity and stability. In depicting this invisible border of human subjectivity, Kristeva draws upon the symbols of the Oedipal Complex as set forth by Freud in *Moses and Monotheism* and *Totem and Taboo.*

In these works, Freud explains the cultural prohibitions of parricide and incest by means of a myth of origins. According to this myth, the father of a primeval horde provokes the jealousy and resentment of his sons due to the attention he receives from their mother. The sons kill the father, and then, seized with guilt, restore paternal authority, now invested with the strong "taboos of totemism," taboos against murder and incest. For Freud, these prohibitions are evidence of the instinctual drives of all humans, drives that form the unconscious substratum of a person and negatively impact his/her conscious behavior.[22]

Although Kristeva accepts the basic thesis of this myth, she differs from Freud in two respects, i.e. in respect to his designation of these drives as instincts and to his evaluation of the drives as always negative. In respect to the former, in placing these drives within the tensions of semiotic/symbolic interaction, Kristeva is, like most poststructuralists, asserting the primary role of language in all knowledge. As Nietzsche insisted, our knowledge of reality is always perspectival, interpreted through the grid of culture and carried through the medium of language. Thus, given Kristeva's understanding of language as a signifying practice, the drives of murder and incest are not outside language, located in a natural sphere untainted by culture, but neither are they outside nature, located in a cultural sphere untainted by the materiality of human becoming. By placing the impulses of murder and incest in the "in-between" of the semiotic and the symbolic, Kristeva is attempting to subvert the nature/culture distinction. One way she alerts us to this is by reference to the "materiality of language."[23]

Second, although Kristeva credits Freud and his structuralist followers with a helpful exposition of the function of sacrifice in preventing wholesale murder, she differs from them in placing more emphasis on the impulse of incest and its alternative history of catharsis, including that which incites human creativity and psychological health. For Kristeva, incest is tied to the prohibitions of purity and cathartic function of abjection. In examining this more closely than her predecessors, she exposes the impure "remainders" of the "clean and proper body," and shifts her understanding of the "mother's body" from some "primeval essence" to an "unnamable otherness" which "like a lining, more secret and invisible" is woven of "fright and repulsion" as well as "desire."[24] The "confrontation with the feminine" in *Powers of Horror*, is an encounter with that which is neither subject nor object, but abject. And the metaphor of the mother's body shifts from that of semiotic nondifferentiation to that which is ejected from cultural systems in order to maintain stable structures and borders.

In examining the logic of exclusion that calls forth the abject, Kristeva turns to the work of anthropologist Mary Douglas, who found "in the human body the prototype of that translucid being constituted by society as symbolic system."[25] While resisting the reductionism of an anthropology that reduces the symbolic system to cause and the individual to an effect, Kristeva uses the body metaphor as a way of understanding the subject within his/her invisible substratum of becoming. Body then is not only the "in-between" of nature and culture, it is also that which mediates between a "speaking subject" and his/her context of signification.

The body, like the social-symbolic system, excludes that which threatens or defiles it, but without total success. The rejected substance (called abject) doesn't disappear, but hovers over the subject as both threat and generating power. Some kinds of abjection, like decay, infection, disease, and a corpse, threaten the body from without. Other kinds, like menstrual blood and feces, threaten it from within. But whether external or internal to the body, all these defilements share an affinity with the mother. Whether associated through a corporeal substance like blood or through a corporeal act like toilet training, these abjects evoke the present/absence of the mother's body. They are the frightening, but desired phantasms of the limits.

These polluting elements are thus "remainders" or fragments of totalizing thought that escape the confines of thought to threaten its sovereignty.

> But here is perhaps the essential point: the remainder appears to be coextensive with the entire architecture of non-totalizing thought. In its view there is nothing that is everything; nothing is exhaustive, there is a residue in every system—in cosmogony, food ritual, and even sacrifice, which deposits, through ashes for instance, ambivalent remains. A challenge to our mono-theistic and mono-logical universes such a mode of thinking apparently needs the ambivalence of remainder if it is not to become enclosed within One single-level symbolics, and thus always posit a non-object as polluting as it is reviving—defilement and genesis.[26]

Within "mono-theistic and mono-logical universes," the remainder or abject is seen only as threat, as a defilement of the sovereign One and thereby something to be expelled. The "ambivalence of remainder" is that quality of the abject which resists this univocal meaning, and in its doubleness as both threat and generative power, continues to infect the logic of the One. Thus, mono-logical systems, by definition, need to rid the abject of its ambivalence, to tame it through absorption or eliminate it through expulsion. Such an abject, translated into the sociohistorical reality of patriarchal structure, is woman.[27]

But before surmising that abjection, even though maternally connoted and historically enacted in the experience of women, applies *only* to women and *equally* to all women, Kristeva goes on to argue that the abject is not necessarily female or male, but rather is anyone or anything identified with cultural remainders. It is not Jocasta, she argues, but

Oedipus, who is the abject of classical Greek culture. Oedipus the King is a tragic figure, one who acts out his desires of parricide and incest in ignorance. He knows "how to unveil logical enigmas,"[28] but doesn't know that he has killed his father and married his mother. In this discovery, he becomes the abject, exiled from family, city, and throne, and forever marked with the castration or wound of blindness. "Blinding is thus an image of splitting; it marks, on the very body, the alternation of the self and clean into the defiled—the scar taking the place of a revealed and yet invisible abjection. Of abjection considered as invisible. In return for which city-state and knowledge can endure."[29]

This scar, while not literally inscribed on all bodies, is nonetheless, the sign of all "speaking subjects" by virtue of their recognition of incompleteness and dependence on the other.

> Our eyes can remain open provided we recognize ourselves as always already altered by the symbolic—by language. Provided we hear in language—and not in the other, not in the other sex—the gouged-out eye, the wound, the basic incompleteness that conditions the indefinite quest of signifying concatenations. That amounts to joying in the truth of self-division [abjection/sacred].[30]

Therefore, given that the abject, the "other," is internal to the self, it can neither be domesticated nor expelled. Its persistent ambivalence must be addressed.

While this statement provides a preliminary definition of the "speaking subject" as one who accepts his/her mortality, even "joys" in it, it does even more. It also provides a clue to a dangerous perversion of this process of evoking joy through wounds, a perversion exemplified in the novels and pamphlets of a twentieth-century fascist, Louis-Ferdinand Celine.

Fascinated by the insights and emotive force of Celine's novels, Kristeva nonetheless struggles with the relation between the "jouissance" of these writings and the author's anti-Semitism. She begins by admitting that Celine, in his attempts to address the "crippling constraints of a society ruled by monotheistic symbolism and its political and legal repercussions,"[31] was potentially a writer of abjection. He knew the anguish of symbolic systems which, through their elitism and moralistic ideology, emasculated the masses. And he knew the delirium of a desire for what had been repressed—a fantasy of pure rhythm, joy, and emotion.

But Celine's writing of this "economy of anguish and joy" that was potentially the source of a creative, transformative power, became instead the source of a vicious, diabolical war against the abject of twentieth-century Europe—the Jewish people. How did this happen? How did the harnessing of emotion so necessary for the therapeutic advance of individuals or cultures become instead the motivating force for a reign of terror?

Kristeva begins her answer to this question in the final pages of *Powers of Horror*, but then continues to wrestle with it in *Tales of Love* and *Strangers to Ourselves*. And even though her position remains consistent in some respects, she does along the way alter her definition of terms and her evaluation of what contributes to a healthy mode of subjectivity and what detracts from it. Central to her argument along this tortuous route is an insight made at the onset—beginning with *Powers of Horror*—that Celine failed, not by releasing anguish into symbolic certitude but by refusing to recognize the sacredness or transcendence of the remainders of such structures, and thereby calling for their elimination. By succumbing to his hatred for the Jews (and secondarily, for women), Celine fell into a delirium for "rhythm, drive, the feminine"—for that undifferentiated wholeness which is the *exclusionary opposite* of the old structures. In this retreat from the ternary qualities of reality to a binary logic of structure and antistructure, he brought about a new symbolic order, more totalizing, oppressive, and vicious than that which had gone before. Celine's writings did release the powerful, emotive forces of the semiotic into the constrictive structures of his day, but only to secure another oppressive structure through the sacrifice of over six million people.[32]

While in her earlier work, Kristeva applauds the rejuvenating effects of poetic language and follows this with a brief, passing remark regarding its potential for co-optation; here, in a later work, she faces this possibility head on. And when she does, she discovers the other side of poetic spontaneity and style—its potential for acting out in history the "deadliest of fantasies"—the extermination of people who personify the qualities of cultural abjection.

The question then becomes how one is to avoid such horror—that of Celine's fear of the abject as well as the horror of his response, for his anti-Semiticism is but one version of the binary logic of totalizing/totalitarian thinking responsible for a host of atrocities committed throughout the history of Western culture. Kristeva's search for an answer to these devastating "unthinkables" opens up possibilities not widely recognized among French poststructuralists—possibilities for an alternative "ontology of relatedness" which is both ethical and religious. Therefore, in pursuing this question further—particularly as it pertains to the history of Jewish and Christian religious traditions, we embark in the final section of this chapter into the territory of aesthetic limits and the sacred.

"Blessed Loving Madness" and the Textual Transgressions of the Sacred

So far, in presenting Kristeva's critique of anesthesized subjects in technological society, we have followed her arguments for the linguisticality of subjectivity, for language as a dynamic signifying practice of three interactive dispositions, and for the "third term" of these dispositions as a key to the formation of healthy "speaking subjects." In her early work, Kristeva argued that this limit, then called the "thetic," modulated the competing forces of the semiotic and symbolic through a process of catharsis. Turning to psychoanalytic analysis, she stipulated two forms of catharsis—that of sacrifice and that of art—as effective in warding off the destructive effects of murder and incest, modulating the forces of "thanatos" and "eros." Poetic language was presented as a form of art that not only reestablished the social-symbolic order for a "speaking subject," but did so through positive transformative effects.

In *Powers of Horror*, Kristeva addresses more directly the problematic of cathartic acts that not only fail to promote healthy modes of subjectivity, but, in accessing the powers of "thanatos" and "eros," channel them into terrifying modes of personal and social destruction. If "madness" is a site of "decentering" or "depresentation" of the stable self or society because of its responsiveness to the primary impulses of the semiotic, then madness can be a force for devastation or for dancing. It can lead to psychosis and fascism or to artistic creativity and mystical ecstasy. The unrelenting call of Kristeva's later writing is to "speak" the subtle mechanisms or micro-practices through which a subject is led into one direction or the other.

In thinking through this problematic, Kristeva is drawn to the metaphor of the body as the site within which the drama of the "speaking subject" is enacted. If one equates the signifying process to the dynamic becoming of an embodied self, then the body, like language, has a ternary quality. The semiotic chora is that unnameable complex of impulses and drives (called motility by phenomenologists), which, like unconscious currents in psychic and cultural life gather in waves of "thanatos" and "eros" and are carried throughout the drama of human life. The symbolic is the structure beset by such waves, the codes and practices of "normality" and "truth" that give form and definition to the body, resisting its collapse into undifferentiated chaos. And the thetic is the liminal zone, the orifices of the body through which substances enter or are eliminated. This zone is the site of alterity for bodily "remainders," the place of their reactive movement within the self or between the self and its wider environment.

In her depiction of the "fortified castle" of the "clean and proper body," Kristeva describes the cathartic process by which a self maintains or reestablishes psychic and social stability. This process is the expulsion of the abject—those substances that defile the body and cause a breakdown of distinctions between subject and object. In Celine's compulsion to set up the pure law of fascism, he had to exterminate the "defiling" elements of his society. He had to sacrifice the Jewish people. In so doing, the abject became object—an object hated with a vehemence not understandable in terms of rational, conscious intention. It was a hatred fed by the paranoia of a beleagered psychic and social symbolic structure. And its consequences are so devastating as to be the "unthinkable" or "unthought" of twentieth-century Western culture.

When Kristeva turns to the ethical and religious as a disposition of the body that counteracts the forces of stagnant stability as well as destructive modes of catharsis, she does so by articulating the dynamic of an "open personality," imaged as the "wounded body" of a "speaking, loving subject." In this section, we will trace her development of this wounded body as it emerged in the religious imagination of Jewish and Christian communities, and relates to a reinterpretation of the "mother's body" in the Oedipal structure of psychoanalytic thought. These together verge on the ethical, that is, for Kristeva, a mode of transgressive love opening up creative possibilities of human becoming.

When one surveys Kristeva's writings for those places where transgression is used in conjunction with religion, we find these two terms not always compatible. Sometimes religion—particularly monotheistic religion—is analogous to other systems of science which reify the subject, making it immune to the creative possibilities of transgressive texts.[33] One way of accomplishing this is through a "cure," that is, through the attempted expulsion of anything that defiles or infects the self. Another way is through anesthesizing the wounds of life, by paralyzing the emotions and immunizing the self from all affective experience.[34] Either way, religion as cure or anesthesia is part of the problem rather than a means of therapeutic change.[35]

In wrestling with alternative modes of religiosity that promote a "loving, speaking subject," Kristeva focuses after 1980 on two types of monotheism—Judaism and Christianity. And although at first she privileges the latter, making Christianity superior to ancient Hebrew religion, she later brings some corrective to this bias and sets the two traditions on a more equal footing. For her, the kind of religion that has positive transgressive force is one in which the self recognizes the "otherness" of its own "wretchedness and glory," and through that recognition, reaches out to the "other" in hospitality and love.[36] This type of religion, originating in Western culture in the discourses of Greek 'eros' and Hebrew 'havad,' finds its fulfillment first within the fringes of Christianity and later within the fringes of modern culture in the writings of the avant-garde.

In order to trace this mode of religiosity in its specificity through history, one must first return to *Powers of Horror*. And there, as mentioned earlier, Kristeva argues that human identity begins in crisis. Such crises—whether spoken of today as the "unthinkable" of the Nazi Holocaust, the death of God, or the more private crises that result in depression and melancholy—are all symbolized as a violent break of the self from the "mother's body," a break which within primary narcissism inflicts a "wound." This wound, in turn, provokes a desire for healing and yet can never fully be cured.

In her first venture into Judaism, particularly in its response to this primal wound, Kristeva draws primarily from Hebrew Bible texts that emphasize the codes of purity. Beginning with Noah's sacrifice of clean beasts and fowls as an offering to his God, the codes of clean/unclean are expanded to include three categories of abomination: food taboos, sickness and death (including the corpse), and the feminine body and incest.[37] Kristeva traces these abominations through the writings of the Pentateuch and the Prophets in order to show how the elaboration and strengthening of prohibitions in ancient Israel gradually provided a counterbalance to earlier forms of sacrifice.[38] The result of this development of law was a loss of the sacredness of "remainders," as all abjects became objects and succumbed to the sovereignty of the "One."

> A religion of abomination overlays a religion of the sacred. It marks the exit of religion and the unfolding of morals; or leading back the One that separates and unifies, not to the fascinated contemplation of the sacred, from which its separates, but to the very device that it ushers in: logic, abstraction, rules of systems and judgments. When the victim is changed into an abomination, a deep qualitative change takes place: the religion that ensues, even if it continues to harbor sacrifice, is no longer a sacrificial religion. It tempers the fascination of murder; it gets around its desire by means of the abomination it associates with any act of incorporation and rejection of an object, thing or living being. What you sacrifice by swallowing, like what you suppress by rejecting, nourishing mother or corpse, are merely pre-texts of the symbolic relation that links you to Meaning. Use them to give existence to the One, but do not make them sacred in themselves. Nothing is sacred outside of the One. At the limit, everything that remains, all remainders, are abominable.[39]

In contrast to this externalizing or rejection of the abject, Christianity created a different "speaking subject" through an "interiorization of abjection," an acknowledgement of an everpresent impurity within the self. Quoting from Mark 15, Kristeva suggests as a paradigmatic text of the early Christian movement the following passage of "internalized abjection." "There is nothing from without a man, that entering into him can defile him: but things which come out of him those are they that defile him."[40] The "split subject" of Christianity thus knows him/herself to be a "divided and contradictory being," one who no longer attributes defilement to something external but rather to "the error within one's own thoughts and speech."[41]

The symbol which addresses this problematic of "interiorized abjection," leading it through a process of sublimation to transformative effects of human becoming is the "body of Christ." This body, which one "eats" in the ritual of Eucharist is a cathartic mode of redemption.

> Purifying, redeeming all sins, it punctually and temporarily gives back innocence by means of communion. To eat and drink the flesh and blood of Christ means, on the one hand, to transgress symbolically the Levitical prohibitions, to be symbolically satiated . . . and to be reconciled with the substance dear to paganism. By the very gesture, however, that corporealizes or incarnates speech, all corporeality is elevated, spiritualized, and sublimated. Osmosis . . . takes place between the spiritual and the substantial, the corporeal and the signifying—a heterogeneity that cannot be divided back into its components.[42]

Thus Kristeva finds in the Christian conception of the "body of Christ" an understanding of heterogeneity or "ambiguity of the flesh" that sees the redemptive possibilities of inner impurity. Instead of experiencing one's "wounds," that is, one's suffering and anguish, as a state of "debt or want" leading to a possessive appetite, wounds can create through sublimation a state of plentitude, one of hospitality and of "being for the other."[43]

This possibility within Christianity, while available to all its devotees, is not claimed by all. In fact, the whole history of the Church reveals that law, condemnation, debt, and punishment are common effects of Christian practice. And the use of one's wounds as source/resource of love is only on the fringes of Christian religion.

> For only on the fringes of mysticism, or in rare moments of Christian life, can the most subtle trans-

gression of law, that is to say, the enunciation of sin in the presence of the One, reverberate not as a denunciation but as the glorious counterweight to the inquisitorial fate of confession . . . Even during the most odious times of the Inquisition, art provided sinners with the opportunity to live, openly and inwardly apart, the joy of their dissipation set into signs: painting, music, words.[44]

At the fringes, in the margins of society and of established religion, the signs of jouissance still break forth through the "speaking subject," and such signs—poetry, painting, music, sculpture—manifesting an alternative mode of catharsis from sacrifice, lead to alternative modes of human becoming.[45]

If *Powers of Horror* unmasks a dangerous mode of catharsis and suggests another way, Kristeva's more recent writing points to places in the history of Western religions where art has served this positive, cathartic purpose. And in specifying the sites of such "holy madness," she draws attention to other possibilities in Judaism as well as Christianity.

In *Tales of Love*, instead of focusing on the development of purity laws in ancient Hebrew religion, Kristeva turns to texts which she construes as preparatory for an amatory speech that later blossoms within Christian mysticism. And the text that serves as the "very dawn of lyrical poetry" and thereby makes possible the "transference of the subject to the other" is that of the biblical "Song of Songs." In this poignant amorous discourse, the "wounds" of love differ both from the abstract ideality of Platonic love and the "pathetic and enthusiastic mistique of orgiastic love germane to pagan worship."[46] Instead, this is a dialogue of "tension and jouissance," not communication, but invocation.

> Whether the speaking subject, insofar as he is a loving subject, is in a permanent state of flight with regard to his addressee; whether he calls him, precedes him, answers him, follows him, without ever uniting with him except in the synthesis of the choruses that break up into the two parts of a duet—such a dynamic reveals, at the very heart of monotheism, at least two motions. The first amounts to the following: through love, I posit myself as subject for the speech of the one who subdues me—the Master. The subjection is

amorous, it supposes a reciprocity, even a priority for the sovereign's love . . . At the same time, and this is the second motion, in amorous dialogue I open up to the other, I welcome him in my loving swoon, or else I absorb him in my exaltation, I identify with him. With those two motions, the premises of *ecstasy* [of one's going out of oneself] and of *incarnation*, insofar as it is the ideal becoming body, are set within the amorous incantation of the Song of Songs.[47]

The invocation of the "other," taking one outside of oneself and making ambiguous the boundaries of self and other as well as spirit and flesh, is a quality of this love—a love among humans and a love between the human and the divine.

In Kristeva's growing awareness of the richness and profundity of the Jewish tradition, she includes in her next book, *Strangers to Ourselves*, a story that she considers equal in insight to some core images of the Christian tradition. The Hebrew Bible story of Ruth is an account of a foreigner who achieved status and honor in the Jewish community as participant in the lineage of David. In so doing, this story reveals a complexity of Jewish law and sovereignty, the paradox of foreignness at its core.

Ruth the foreigner is there to remind those unable to read that the divine revelation often requires a lapse, the acceptance of radical otherness, the recognition of a foreignness that one might have tended at the very first to consider the most degraded. This was not an encouragement to deviate or to proselytize but an invitation to consider the fertility of the other . . . Perhaps damaged, worried at any rate, that sovereignty opens up—through the foreignness that founds it—to the dynamics of a constant, inquisitive, and hospitable questioning, eager for the other and for the self as "other."[48]

Ruth, then, within the ternary dispositions of ancient Judaism, becomes the "double," the stranger who, by resisting full and complete assimilation, initiates the "constant quest for welcoming and going beyond the other in oneself."[49]

The Apostle Paul, one of the primary figures in the originating events of the Christian tradition, in breaking from "the nationalism of Jewish communities," was still in continuity with that strand of the Jewish tradition represented by Ruth and David.[50] In establishing the Christian *Ecclesia* as an alternative community to national and ethnic groups, Paul helped create a "community of foreigners," one which rested upon an alternative "logic of subjectivity." Relating the foreigner without to a foreignness within, this logic sees within the community and within its individual members a "wound," an imperfection or strangeness that is the spur for a journey of "love for the other."[51] In this way, "the body of Christ" became a primary image for the community. Remembering its own "wretchedness and glory" through the ritual of Eucharist, Christian devotees know themselves to be in perpetual process, encouraged to go beyond themselves in hospitality to the stranger.[52]

One of Kristeva's most powerful depictions of this body in the history of Christian art is her interpretation of Hans Holbein's painting, "The Body of the Dead Christ in the Tomb."[53] In contrast to other paintings of Christ during the late Middle Ages which relieved "the weight of human grief" through signs of life or resurrection, Holbein's Christ is an unadorned representation of death in all its tragedy and bleakness.

Yet in proposing such a vision, in painting so realistically the death that threatens every person throughout life, Holbein's painting does not lead to a tired and cynical atheism, but to rejuvenated life, a form of dancing. It invites us, "to change the Christly tomb into a living tomb, to participate in the painted death and thus include it in our own life, in order to live with it and make it live."[54]

Reminding her readers of the friendship between Holbein the Younger and Erasmus, Kristeva suggests that this picture of Christ and therefore of all humans is a visual image presented in words by Erasmus in his book, *In Praise of Folly*. It is only by acknowledging one's own folly, by looking death in the face, and accepting its risks that the human moves toward true dignity and fullness of life. To "be swallowed up by death, or perhaps to see it in its slightest, dreadful beauty, as the limit inherent in life," brings about a "grating irony"—the emergence of "the erotic vitality of the self," freed from the images and identity of the self as a self-assured, self-constituted, and triumphant being. The "body of Christ" in its anguish and pain is in this sense then also a body of "jouis-sance."[55]

How then does this sacred body of the Christian tradition relate to the "mother's body" of psychoanalytic discourse and finally, to the "transgressive corporeality" of an alternative ethical and religious imagination? We conclude this chapter with a suggestion regarding the interrelation of all these bodies.

As noted earlier, Kristeva vacillates between associating the "mother's body" with the semiotic chora or with the thetic, the limit between the semiotic and symbolic. In the first designation, when she speaks of the mother's body as a force of chaotic drives typified by "thanatos" and "eros," Kristeva falls into a form of binary thinking that she elsewhere criticizes. In this mode of thought, the thetic—torn between the violent forces of chaos and structure—either dissolves, allowing for the unrestrained expression of primal forces, or becomes rigid and impermeable, fortifying a structure that in its fixity, re-presses and oppresses the "other." Either way, whether through total collapse or total control, the thetic loses its resilience and thereby its potential for moderating "reciprocal violence" and creating positive, transformative changes in the psychic and social life of modern culture.

So Kristeva is, throughout her writings, interested in the retention of the "limit" as a permeable membrane which, through the catharsis of art, not only maintains social stability but also transforms it. And one of the images she uses to depict this limit that neither dissolves nor becomes reified in the tensions of life is that of the "mother's body."

This image initially emerges in her reinterpretation of the Oedipal Complex. While Freud and Lacan both accepted the "mother's body" as object of desire, Kristeva in *Powers of Horror*, creates the term "abject" in order to shift the connotation of the maternal body from that of object to that of limit, that is, neither subject nor object. And she does so by tying this body to the "remainders" of cultural codes, remainders which are expelled but not fully exterminated. The "mother's body" then as the waste or residue of cultural codes is the third term of ternary thinking, a term with radical social, political, economic, and ethical implications.

Some of these implications are explored by Kristeva in her essay, "Stabat Mater." Here, the image of the Virgin Mother is contrasted with Kristeva's own experience of being pregnant, giving birth, and relating to a child. In setting these up in juxtaposition to each other, Kristeva is attempting to "write" the "mother's body" as a limit of redemptive possibility.

She begins by chronicling the development of the image of the Virgin Mother within the Christian religious imagination. This mother, serving as the "focal point of men's desires and aspirations," is either an impossible ideal or a whore.[56] Put in terms of Hegelian philosophy, woman is either "immediately universal," that is, untainted, nonsexual being, or "immediately particular," that is, sexual and fallen.[57] What is left out or covered over in this myth of the Virgin is the mother's heterogeneity, her nature as a "being of folds, a catastrophe of being that the dialectics of the trinity and its supplements would be unable to subsume."[58] This third term as a subversion of the universal/particular dialectic, is the image of the Mother as singular and heterogeneous.

This body, implicit within the myth of the Virgin, becomes explicit in the experience of those who give birth.

> The unspoken doubtless weighs first on the maternal body: as no signifier can uplift it without leaving a remainder, for the signifier is always meaning, communication, or structure, whereas a woman as mother would be, instead, a strange fold that changes culture into nature, the speaking into biology. Although it concerns every woman's body, the heterogeneity that cannot be subsumed in the signifier nevertheless explodes violently with pregnancy [the threshold of culture and nature] and the child's arrival [which extracts women out of her oneness and gives her the possibility—but not the certainty—of reaching out to the other, the ethical].[59]

Thus, the mother's body for Kristeva is a "crossroads being," a being of relatedness in which the "other" internal to her in pregnancy becomes an "other" external to her in the birth of a child. And this "other," (a "gap" within oneself as well as between the self and other) is both source of pain and of irrepressible jouissance. Such "otherness," as frightening and yet joyous, the "unending germination" of life, is none other than the sacred. If "Christ's body" is a wounded being inviting participation in those wounds as part of a journey toward life, then the "mother's body," holding the otherness of death and life within her, is the site within which such new life actually occurs.

This mother, unlike the image of the pure virgin as well as the erotic images of fertility goddesses, leads neither to patriarchal structure nor to erotic indulgence but to ethics, and in particular, to a "herethics." Concluding "Stabat Mater" as she did her dissertation with a turn to ethics, Kristeva suggests that for the heterogeneous mother, "remainders" are a sacred other, eliciting a desire for the becoming of both mother and child in the resilient dynamics of a "frightening, joying" love. And ethics is the speaking and writing of such sacred remainders.

A question that surfaces throughout Kristeva's writing— one that is a catalyst for her own quest of a healthy subjectivity—is that of images or stories that speak the dynamics of human becoming. We suffer, she says, from an "abolition of psychic space," a space that is "drowned in a cascade of false images (from social roles to the media), hence deprived of substance or place."[60] The antidote to this is not the reinstating of an old psychic space, the reconstruction of "a clean and proper self" built on "the machinery of projections and identifications" that rely on neuroses for reinforcement. Instead, it is the creation of a new subject, one that speaks in "unstable, open, undecidable" spaces, speaking the cathartic discourse of love.

This discourse—"Music, film, novel. Polyvalent, undecidable, infinite."[61]—does not relieve the psyche of its crises, but it does turn these crises into a "work in progress," a work of renewal, of rebirth, of youth. The textual transgression of the sacred for Kristeva is the ongoing, painful transgression of the "clean and proper body" submerged in the false images of technological society, a transgression that invites one to acknowledge his/her wounds, and through the "wounds of love" begin the process of being reborn, of coming back to loving relations, of coming back to life. The erotic is an aesthetic limit, the liminal space in our culture and era, not just of any body, but of the heterogeneous body of resilient relations, the body of the mother. We are, each one of us, in all our differences, that body. And its actualization is in the transgression of our "speaking"—a transgression of "blessed loving madness."

Notes

1. Julia Kristeva, *Black Sun: Depression and Melancholia*, trans. Leon S. Roudiez (New York: Columbia University Press, 1989), 87.

2. Julia Kristeva, *Powers of Horror: An Essay on Abjection*, trans. Leon S. Roudiez (New York: Columbia Univ. Press, 1982), 210.

3. Julia Kristeva, *Revolution of Poetic Language*, trans. Margaret Waller (New York: Columbia University Press, 1984), 21–4.

4. Julia Kristeva, *Desire in Language: A Semiotic Approach to Literature and Art*, trans. Thomas Gora, Alice Jardine, and Leon S. Roudiez, ed. Leon S. Roudiez (New York: Columbia University Press, 1980), 133.

5. Ibid., 283–4.

6. Julia Kristeva, *Tales of Love*, trans. Leon S. Roudiez (New York: Columbia University Press, 1987), 8.

7. For Jacques Lacan's reinterpretation of Freud's theory of the development of the "ego," see *Ecrits: A Selection*, trans. Alan Sheridan (New York: W. W. Norton, 1977).

8. In "The Adolescent Novel," Kristeva depicts this "open structure" personality as one which maintains a "renewable identity through interaction with another" and relates this flexible structure to the ambiguities of adolescence. See *Abjection, Melancholia and Love: The Work of Julia Kristeva*, ed. John Fletcher and Andrew Benjamin (New York: Routledge, 1990), 9–23.

9. Kristeva, *Poetic Language*, 49–51. Note the analogy between this "split subject" and the "gap" between the touching/being touched explored by Merleau-Ponty. This gap is both internal to the self and between selves.

10. Ibid., 83.

11. Rene Girard, *Violence and the Sacred*, trans. Patrick Gregory (Baltimore, Md.: Johns Hopkins University Press, 1977), 26.

12. Ibid., 93.

13. Kristeva, *Poetic Language*, 78.

14. Ibid., 79. Also see p. 136 of *Desire in Language* where she equates poetic language to the prohibition of incest.

15. Ibid., 79.

16. Ibid., 83.

17. Kristeva, *Desire in Language*, 71–2.

18. Ibid., 86.

19. Kristeva, *Poetic Language*, 232–4.

20. Ibid., 233.

21. Ibid., 234.

22. Kristeva, *Powers of Horror*, 56–7.

23. Kristeva, *Revolution in Poetic Language*, 103.

24. Kristeva, *Powers of Horror*, 58.

25. Ibid, 66.

26. Ibid., 76.

27. This helps to explain the impulse within Western culture to designate women either as virgins or as whores, that is, Mary the mother of Jesus or Mary Magdalene. Kristeva's call for a "herethics" based on the "mother's desire" resists both domestication and rejection.

28. Ibid., 83.

29. Ibid., 84.

30. Ibid., 88.

31. Ibid., 179.

32. Ibid., 178–80.

33. Kristeva, *Poetic Language*, 58–9.

34. Kristeva, *Black Sun*, 87.

35. One must distinguish here between the healing process, which is of paramount concern to Kristeva as a practicing

psychoanalyst, and "cure," which in poststructuralist discourse is a metaphor for the process by which one purifies oneself of the "wounds" of suffering and anguish. Such purifying, as we have just noted, has oppressive effects.

36. Julia Kristeva, *Strangers to Ourselves*, trans. Leon S. Roudiez (New York: Columbia Univ. Press, 1991), 122.

37. Kristeva, *Powers of Horror*, 92–3.

38. Ibid., 110. Kristeva argues that earlier forms of Hebrew religion, in reviewing the sacrificial victim as much as fearing it, resisted the strict binarism of clean/unclean logic.

39. Ibid., 111.

40. Ibid., 113–4.

41. Ibid., 116–7.

42. Ibid., 119–20.

43. Ibid., 123–9.

44. Ibid., 131.

45. Ibid., 132.

46. Kristeva, *Tales of Love*, 97.

47. Ibid., 93.

48. Kristeva, *Strangers to Ourselves*, 75.

49. Ibid., 76.

50. Ibid., 79.

51. Ibid., 84.

52. Ibid., 85.

53. Kristeva, *Black Sun*, 107.

54. Ibid., 113.

55. Ibid., 137.

56. Kristeva, *Tales of Love*, 245.

57. Ibid., 248.

58. Ibid., 260.

59. Ibid., 259.

60. Kristeva, *Tales of Love*, 373.

61. Ibid., 263.

CHAPTER FIVE

Transgressive Corporeality as the Imaginary of Theology

> The metaphoric postmodern can best be described as a fundamental ontology of the body where metaphysics, now dismembered and disassembled, can be "rewritten" as pure somatology, as the deciphering of the "aesthetic" or sensate markings we know as world and as culture.
>
> —Carl A. Raschke, "Fire and Roses"

The Theological Imagination in Theologies of Construction

The "theological imagination" has become in the last couple of decades a key phrase in contemporary Christian theology. As used by Gordon Kaufman in his exploration of theological method, the term "imagination" reflects a critical turning point in the epistemology of modern scholarship. Veering away from the claims of a traditional metaphysics rooted in revelation as well as a romantic psychology of religion based on experience, proponents of the theological imagination emphasize the role of culture and language as the necessary and irreplacable lens through which all reality is known, including those dimensions of reality commonly called sacred or divine.[1]

This turn, prompted by Kant's first two critiques, *The Critique of Pure Reason* and *The Critique of Practical Reason*, and continued in a more radically historical fashion by Karl Marx, Sigmund Freud, and Friedrich Nietzsche (often called the "masters of suspicion"), has placed as great an emphasis on ethics as on epistemology. In the case of Kant, his critique of Cartesian rationalism was interwoven with a deep concern for human moral action, and in particular, for a new theoretical basis for such action. In the work of the nineteenth-century "masters of suspicion," this intertwining of epistemology and ethics continued, despite widely divergent methods and results.

Gordon Kaufman also insists on the linkage of epistemology and ethics, and does so through a pragmatic evaluation of the function of theological symbols. In his view, the dominant symbols of the Christian faith are "true" to the extent that they perform two functions, that they relativize all prevailing images or concepts of God and that they humanize the faith community through "promoting and enhancing human development and fulfillment."[2] True knowledge then is inextricably linked to true moral action. For the proponents of a theological imagination, one cannot be had without the other.

This study of transgressive corporeality as a theological enterprise begins with the basic premises of the theological imagination. It begins by accepting the necessary role of culture and language as the medium of knowledge, and by affirming the intertwining of "true" knowledge with "true" moral relations. In addition, it also draws these insights from the turning points reflected in the work of Kant and the "masters of suspicion."

And yet, this study is not simply an elaboration of the theological imagination as defined by its major theorists. For in drawing from the critique of Nietzsche, and more implicitly from Kant, this work brings into the theological conversation somewhat different aspects of their writing and thereby sets up the problematic of contemporary theology in a different way. In addition, this problematic is addressed through a trajectory of thinkers—from Merleau-Ponty to Foucault to Kristeva—not yet given full attention by contemporary theologians of construction.

Therefore, before proceeding to a summation of the insights of our three major theorists, it is important first to review the nature of the problematic of transgressive corporeality as set forth in chapter 1. Aside from bringing the basic premises of that problematic back into focus, this review may also suggest some of the similarities and differences between the approach of this study and that of other theorists of the theological imagination.

The first similarity as well as difference is in the use of the writings of Friedrich Nietzsche. Both theologians of construction and poststructuralists applaud Nietzsche's insistence on the historical and thereby perspectival nature of knowledge. In addition, they agree on the dangers of a "will-to-truth" which attempts to confine the irreducible elements of existence to a fixed, unitary, and universal truth. Although their tactics and styles of writing differ dramatically, both types of theology are engaged in processes of "unmasking," that is, of making visible those forms of the "will-to-truth" which currently operate in our culture, including the relations of exchange upon which they are based and the mechanisms of control through which they operate. In this sense, both theological approaches are deconstructive before they are in any way reconstructive.[3]

But theologians working out of a poststructuralist critique of culture and language take the deconstructive task one step further than their constructivist colleagues. In Mark C. Taylor's critique of hegemonic truths girded in utilitarian relations, he shows the affinity of such truths with modes of binary thinking tied to a transcendental signified, and insists on the primacy of the "limit" as the "nonoriginal origin" or source of theological thinking. Thus, the "a/theological imagination" of Taylor's writing, as a poststructuralist endeavor, is especially incisive in its critique of the structures and subtleties of binary economies of thought and belief, including those perpetrated by certain forms of constructive and secular theologies. Like Nietzsche's dethroning of the idols of the modernist subject, the deconstruction practiced by poststructuralist theologians topples the idols of all projects which consciously or not relax the tensions or alterity of the limit.

The other difference between theologies of construction and poststructuralism involves the role of the sensual in a new theological imagination. Looking back at chapter 1, both Nietzsche and Eco in different time periods and literary styles argue that immutable truths are achieved only through the suppression or oppression of the sensual, that is, those markings of culture subject to the limitations and vicissitudes of finite existence which engage the senses of sight, sound, touch, smell, and taste. Thus, the site for new thinking or reconstruction is just those "sensual remainders" or "sensate markings" of culture that survive the clash between forces of the "will-to-truth" and their opposition.

When "sensual remainders" rather than cognitive concepts are seen as resources for theological thinking, these lead more to an "aesthetics of existence" or "ontology of relatedness" then to a new systematic metaphysics. And the aesthetics being explored by poststructuralist theologians is an aesthetics designed to resist the dualistic thinking of traditional metaphysics. As stated by Nietzsche in *The Birth of Tragedy*, in aesthetics, "the whole opposition between the subjective and objective . . . is altogether irrelevant."[4]

Therefore, given this turn to aesthetics (in our terminology, a turn to the body), the work of Kant continues to be valued as a critical turning point, but now with an emphasis on his third critique as well as the first two. This critique, *The Critique of Judgment* where Kant deals with the "remainders" of his earlier ones, is a treatise on aesthetics. And although the third critique is not directly addressed by this study, it does provide a backdrop for the explorations of our major theorists, and therefore for our own. And the arena of Kant's investigations most pertinent to the sensual remainders of this study is that of the "sublime," as that which is most directly reflective of the dynamics of transgression.[5]

But without further reiteration of this problematic, let us turn to the contributions of Maurice Merleau-Ponty, Michel Foucault, and Julia Kristeva to the enterprise of transgressive corporeality. For in exploring their understandings of the dynamics of embodied existence, we will see more clearly the operations of fixed forms of "will-to-truth" in Western thought and culture, as well as glimpse some emerging alternatives. Our goal is threefold: a depiction of various forms of the "will-to-truth" that violate the body, an articulation of the powers and potentials of the body which resist these truths, and finally, an exploration of the boundary or limit between these conflicting forces—a boundary necessary for the creative well-being of all "bodies." Following our summary of the contributions of these three theorists, we will proceed to evaluate their insights with respect to the sources and directions of contemporary theology.

The Ternary Dispositions of
Embodied Existence

In Merleau-Ponty's turn to the body as a way in which we dwell in the world, he resists the tendency of both empiricism and idealism toward a subject/object split which places all reality on the objective side. Whether one begins, he argues, with "absolute subjectivity" or with "absolute objectivity," the nature of the world remains the same. It remains "defined by the absolute mutual exteriority of its parts," a binary structure of mutually exclusive oppositions subject to full explanation and representation. Merleau-Ponty's "phenomenology of perception" reveals the inadequacy of these approaches and poses an alternative.

His philosophical enterprise, put into the categories of the present study, is a discernment and critique of dominant forms of the Enlightenment "will-to-truth." "Objective thought," in both its empiricist and idealist modes, is blind to tacit relations between subject and object—relations which reveal an ambiguity within both subject and object, and resist full representation. Merleau-Ponty's first contribution to our notion of body is his depiction of body as neither absolute subject nor absolute object, but as a field of practical action in the world, one which spawns ever-shifting modes of identity from within the texture of its relations. Such a body breaks the dualism of subject/object relations by drawing attention to the conditions of subjectivity, the phenomenal field of interaction with "other" entities of existence.

His second contribution, one explored further by Foucault and Kristeva, is his insistence on the plentitude of the "gap" within subjects and between subjects and objects. This gap—sometimes depicted as the "difference" of the knower and the known or as the "transcendence" of the other to the self—is for Merleau-Ponty the source and limit of both knowledge and value. As the "present/absent" quality of all human relations, this gap invites interrogation—animating the sight of the body/seer and calling for a creative response. As suggested earlier in this study, the sirens of knowledge are neither in the projections of the subject nor in the givenness of the object. They are instead within the abyss of difference.

In his later work, as Merleau-Ponty began a shift in focus

from the body of perception to the flesh of language, he depicted "objective thought" in the metaphor of the "gaze of the spectator," a gaze that discovers its truth by ignoring the problems and paradoxes of the world's relations, and then imposes this truth on all others. This gaze violates the body by attempting to confine or fix its meaning according to inner structures or essences.

But even though Merleau-Ponty presents the "spectator's gaze" in the context of a revisioning of language, it is Michel Foucault who ties this gaze to the actual operations of language and traces its history through varying periods of post-Enlightenment culture. By doing this, Foucault not only brings into focus the hidden epistemic relations of different eras, but also succeeds in provoking a negative response. For in seeing the operation of each "will-to-truth" upon the bodies of the European populace, the reader of Foucault's works is offended, sometimes even horrified, and thereby called to actions of resistance against such truths.

As one surveys the operations of the "gaze" throughout the pre-Classical, Classical, and Modern eras of Foucault's histories,[6] body continues to be the site for the intersection of forces within the field of historical existence, but now with two emphases missing from Merleau-Ponty's early work. The first emphasis, moving away from all notions of subjectivity based on consciousness, is the inscription of forces on the body. It is not the self-conscious subject but language that speaks, and it does so in the body's gestures, dreams, and illnesses. Body then is not the physical container of a privatized mind, but a theatre for the play of language, the performance of signs upon the stages of the world.

For Foucault, the freeplay of language, or in Saussure's terms, the disconnection of the signifier from the signified, does not necessarily liberate people. In fact, it usually does the opposite. For once freed from the tyranny of fixed points of reference, bodies are still subject to the control mechanisms of cultural modes of power/knowledges operating through the dynamic of language. Thus, the operation of particular complexes of power/knowledge on bodies, although productive of modes of thinking and being, is largely restrictive and constrictive in respect to the types of rationalities and behaviors produced. And in the shift from the reign of the sovereign in the pre-Classical era to the control mechanisms of micro-practices in modernity, the constrictions become more covert and therefore more powerful. If the soul of a culture is its particular apparatus of power/knowledge, then body virtually becomes imprisoned in the soul. And the "will-to-truth" which confines the body is no longer a conscious force acting upon the self from outside it, but a "panoptical gaze" set up by the structures of a culture's discursive and nondiscursive practices and made effective via the largely unconscious internalization processes of the individual. Reality is still objectified, but now through much more pervasive and subtle means.

In turning to Julia Kristeva's analysis of culture and language, we find this interest in the grip of cultural codes on the body continued, but with a tenacity for hope largely missing in Foucault's writings. Kristeva's work, drawing heavily upon recent psychoanalytic theory as well as anthropological and literary studies, emphasizes the ternary quality of embodied/ linguistic existence, that is, the semiotic, thetic, and symbolic. And because the semiotic and symbolic are each constantly threatening either to absorb or exterminate each other, the thetic or boundary between them plays a crucial role in the development of human beings and cultures.

The thetic, roughly akin to Jacque Lacan's "imaginary," is the means by which identity is shaped and maintained. For Lacan, the imaginary, inaugurated in the mirror stage of a young child's life, is a unification of the fragmented body of the subject through an image that is largely alien and external to her/him. This imaginary, put into effect through the child's interaction with parental figures, is for both Freud and Lacan the scene of the Oedipal Complex. As such, the child (assumed in their theories to be male) attains his identity through a process of desire for the "mother" and violent struggle with the "father" for her attention. Thus, incest and patricide become the catalysts for identity formation—an identity wrought from the negative impulses of lack and murderous desire.[7]

Although Kristeva accepts Lacan's association of the imaginary with a dynamic within language, she revolutionizes his theory by shifting her emphasis from patricide to incest and then giving "love for/by the mother" a new interpretation. For Kristeva, the thetic or boundary between the semiotic and symbolic is activated and maintained through the catharsis of "mother love." And this practice, operating within the poetic texts of avant-garde writers, retains a tensive dynamic between semiotic and symbolic forces, neither allowing the dissolution of the subject into semiotic babblings nor his/her rigidification in symbolic structures.

The thetic then, for Kristeva, is of paramount importance for processes of healthy human development. Without its bursts of nonviolent catharsis, the body loses its ternary quality, retreating into a form of binarism that privileges one term of the semiotic/symbolic dyad, culminating in sometimes subtle but nevertheless always destructive results. Without the modulating influence of the thetic, the body becomes the territory of master/slave relations—relations which demand the depletion or diminishment of the "other" for the sake of the secure identity of the "same." And as exemplified in the writings of Celine, these are relations which wreak havoc upon the "abject" or "unclean" entities of the world, entities such as women, Jews, and all others who threaten the power and prestige of the reigning order.

Thus, in moving toward an understanding of body as a relational complex with a ternary quality, all three theorists presented in this study reject modes of the "will-to-truth" that collapse human existence into a totalizing structure based on pairs of exclusionary oppositions with each side of the pair vying for supremacy. For Merleau-Ponty, the body resists the dichotomy of subject/object relations posed by empiricism or idealism. And the medium through which speaking subjects interact is depicted metaphorically as the primary elements of water and fire. For him, the third term is a dynamic within the field of human relatedness, that is, the "internal animation" of water or the "spark" inciting artistic vision, each prompting the movement of healthy human becoming. For Merleau-Ponty, this "third term," sometimes depicted as the elemental force of "brute, wild Being," emerges out of the field of human relatedness and elicits relations of "co-naissance" or "co-birthing." His aesthetics of existence then is also an alternative "ontology of relatedness," the creative becoming of self and other.

For Foucault, the body is primarily the site for the inscription of power within culture, power that writes itself on the body in ever more subtle and insidious ways. Less sanguine than Merleau-Ponty about the possibilities of "wild Being" for expressions of creativity and loving relations, Foucault emphasizes the mechanisms of control which impede healthy human identity formation. And yet, even for him, just as the processes of objectification of the pre-Classical and Classical eras were disturbed and disrupted by the "remainders" of the reigning power/knowledge complexes, so too the binary economy of humanistic modernity can also be called into question and resisted. And the site of resistance, as alluded to in the *History of Sexuality*, has to do with the sensual, with "bodies and pleasures." The third term or boundary between the inscription of forces on the body and its violent responses is a dynamic within language that speaks a "voluptas pleasure," one of nonpossessive and nondefensive encounters of the self with a respected and valued "other."

But that to which Foucault only alludes, Kristeva explores with great subtlety and diligence. For her, the ternary quality of language and therefore of existence is therapeutic when the third term or thetic operates out of a catharsis of "love for/by the mother." Such catharsis as a dimension of language is put into effect through the works of certain ancient, medieval, and contemporary artists and writers. And yet, because the operation of language as a complex of signifying practices cannot be divorced from all other arenas of human experience, this catharsis has political and religious ramifications as well.

Politically, this burst of "love for/by the mother" resists the temptation of a subject to turn cultural abjects into objects through processes of domestication or elimination. Such abjects or "strangers" to the self, whether internal or external, must be granted their own integrity, and allowed, despite their threat to the secure identity of the subject, to engender a dynamic of "ec-static" human relations, subservient neither to operative structures of the symbolic nor to their semiotic counterparts.

Thus, for Kristeva, these entities of the threshold between the forces of form and chaos in human life can be vehicles of hope when these abjects, as signs of the "mother's desire," give shape to an alternative mode of relatedness. Resisting the violence and mutual destructiveness of a master/slave dialectic, the "sensual remainders" of the threshold can evoke a desire for the "co-birthing" of self and other. In this way, Merleau-Ponty's third term of "wild Being" becomes for Kristeva the catharsis of "wild love." And the embodied enactment of such love in human life is for her the "incarnation of the holy." It is the wellspring of both fright and joy—decentering the subject through the wounds of difference and prompting a catharsis of creative change.

In conclusion, the third term of the ternary dispositions of human life and language for Merleau-Ponty, Foucault, and Kristeva moves from "wild Being" to "voluptas pleasure" to "wild love"—each time dealing in more detail and depth with the operations of the "will-to-truth" that restrict the body, with those forces that resist these operations, and finally with the kind of dynamic between these competing forces of structure and antistructure that prompts creative rather than destructive effects. And it is "wild love" as set forth by Kristeva, building upon the analyses of Merleau-Ponty and Foucault, that becomes the aesthetics of a new "ontology of relatedness," a somatology of the "sensate markings" of culture and world.

The Third Term as "Originary Site" of the Imagination

Having now argued for the ternary quality of embodied existence, and for the importance of a third term which through catharsis allows for healthy modes of creativity in human becoming, we must now ask what this analysis contributes to current issues of theological method. What does this argument avoid, and to what kind of theology might it lead?

Earlier in this study, we depicted philosophy as an interrogation of a "ground," of that invisible substratum of human life upon which edifices of meaning are built. Within a dualistic framework of meaning, this ground is understood as a stable foundation, immune to the vicissitudes of historical existence and serving as an Archimedean point of reference for all formulations of truth. In theology, this enterprise includes all those projects of traditional metaphysics which discover stable foundations within the field of culture and religion and represent these realities in religious language, whether it be the language of God, religious experience, inerrant texts, universal archetypes, or the grammar of religious language.

The initial formulation of the theological imagination entailed a break with such foundationalist enterprises. Not only did pre-Enlightenment notions of revelation lose their authority as self-evident truths, but also Enlightenment notions of reason, and Romantic notions of direct experience came under close scrutiny and critique. Theology, according to the post-Kantian perspective of scholars like Gordon Kaufman, George Lindbeck, and Sallie McFague is an enterprise of analyzing theological language for its effects, and then reconstructing such language to produce those effects valued by the community, whether that community is defined confessionally or as accountable to a wider public.[8]

For these scholars, then, theology as a cultural/linguistic construction, admittedly unhooked from "nature" or the "real," is a tool for the promotion of moral relations within the community of faith and between that community and others. The test of theological truth in this schema is a pragmatic evaluation of the "truth effects" of religious symbols, and the theological task is the challenge of controlling these effects through the reshaping of its dominant symbols. Put in the stark imagery of Foucault's critique, the "panopticon," from the perspective of the most extreme forms of theological pragmatism, is not bad in itself—it simply needs a new supervisor, instilling within the individual cells of the prison an alternative ethic. And what better supervisor might there be than the constructive theologian?

One way of depicting the difference of this study from more blatantly pragmatic interpreters of the theological imagination is through a return to the notion of the ground of philosophy and theology. If both theology and philosophy are the interrogation of the ground of thinking, and this ground is not the fixed foundations of traditional metaphysics, then what is it? And how, in the case of theology, does it get us beyond the present impasse of a nature/culture dichotomy and controlling "panopticism" continued in the methodologies of some modernist modes of theological construction?[9]

Merleau-Ponty, Foucault, and Kristeva, in struggling toward the articulation of a "third term" of the ternary dispositions of existence, present us with the formulation of an alternative "originary site" for philosophical and theological thinking. This site or primal scene of human becoming has three characteristics which distinguish it from the ground of foundationalist projects. First, as set forth by Merleau-Ponty, the site of bodily thinking, akin to the unruly realm of interhuman relations, is not fully present and able to be represented. Rather, it has the quality of a presence/absence, that is, a presence which comes to the fore only against the backdrop of the absent or tacit relations of one's practical action in the world. Therefore, for him, this site is not a stable foundation but a "gap"—the gap within the phenomenon of "touching/being touched," or put otherwise, the difference or transcendence of one self to an other within the field of historical existence.

Merleau-Ponty speaks of this gap as the "inalienable horizon" of the flesh.[10] Foucault speaks of it as the "unthought" entangled within the "warp and woof" of thought.[11] And Kristeva speaks of it as the "abject," "wound," or "remainder" of the "clean and proper body."[12] Although each of these metaphors directs our attention to different facets of this site, they all insist on its irreducibility to full representation. This gap is a limit to symbolic structures, and as its limit, it is near to representation, indeed at its borders, but never fully contained within it.

The second feature of this nonfoundational site is its modus operandi through the powers of attraction or repulsion. Resisting the objectifying gaze of spectator relations, this gap or limit of thought and representation decenters the subject, beckoning her/him to thinking prior to the onset of the subject's conscious projections. One way of stating this is that this site operates through the powers of desire. And such desire, spoken of by Merleau-Ponty and Kristeva as the "phantom of vision," emerges out of the complexity and complicity of human relatedness, fueling the imagination and igniting its fecund powers. The call to thinking from this site is more than a gentle lure. It is the sirens of seduction.

Third, when one investigates the nature of this call as emanating from the liminal zones of the body, one finds a growing association in these three writers between this call and the powers of "eros." And the eros that they depict is not that of binary thinking but of ternary bodily thinking. In the former, eros is a drive for unification with the mother, created out of a lack or need within oneself. It is a yearning for the womb—for that undifferentiated realm of primal drives and feelings which fulfills all wants and satisfies all needs. From the time of Plato to that of Freud and Lacan, this eros emanates out of a primal lack and culminates in a compulsive drive for satiation.[13]

In contrast, the eros of Merleau-Ponty, Foucault, and Kristeva is an ex-centric rather than concentric or unifying force.

Emerging out of the gap or transcendence of one subject to an other within relations of mutual respect and reciprocity, this ex–centric eros continually decenters the subject, but does so as a prelude to the activation of new possibilities. Thus, this eros does not arise out of the lack of the subject, but out of the plentitude of difference operating within the field of historical existence. Through the "eternal recurrence of difference," the boundaries of the body are continually threatened or wounded by the encroachment of an "other" which resists being defined or consumed by the self. This wound then is the vulnerability of an embodied self to others—a vulnerability which, if reciprocated, leads to empathetic engagement whereby the needs of the other become recognized and addressed.[14]

In this way, the eros of the limits of an embodied self is the "corp-o-sant" or spark of atmospheric tensions that acts as a catalyst for creative response and growth. Such eros does not cure the body. It does not reinstate the clear and impermeable boundaries of the "clean and proper" self. Instead, it creates lesions or wounds through which the self maintains a resilient receptivity to the joys and sorrows of the world.[15]

For Merleau-Ponty, the decentering of the body by an "other" is prominent in the experience of painters. Through the dehisience of "wild Being" within the significations of historical existence, the space and light of the world disturbs patterns of normality, prompting a creative breakthrough. Although Foucault, recognizing the insidious mechanisms through which patterns of normality operate, is more skeptical of such breakthroughs, he too affirms a power of eros, spawned within the open game of nondefensive encounters with an other of recognized worth, and decentering the subject through the spur of relational tensions. The catharsis suggested within his *History of Sexuality* is an "aesthetics of existence" whereby relations of intimacy between those of equal freedom and value increase the unsettling pleasure of the "other."

Aside from providing a balance between Merleau-Ponty's optimism and Foucault's pessimism regarding possibilities for the breakthrough of ex-centric eros in human life, Kristeva draws the powers of the erotic more closely to an "aesthetics of signification" by showing its movement within the materiality of language. For her, the "ec-stasy" of eros is not the madness of Celine, who needed to sacrifice Jews and women for a fusion with the mother. Instead, the terrain of madness that Kristeva explores, depicted not as desire *for the mother*, but as *the mother's desire* (le mère qui jouit), is the madness of those at the limits of reason and representation who continually threaten the authority of normative modes of thinking and being through the generative power of eros.

To speak this "madness," this "blessed, loving madness," is to unleash the "unspeakable" remainders of the limits into the rationalities of the symbolic. It is the madness sought after by Adrienne Rich in her quest for speaking woman's desire within the confines of patriarchy. To do this, she must have "The freedom of the wholly mad/to smear and play with her madness/write with her fingers dipped in it."[16] It is as well the madness of Merle, a woman of irregular origins and unruly behavior, who called into question the exploitive structures of the sugarcane industry in her beloved island of Bournehills.[17] And it is the madness of a young French girl and her Chinese lover challenging the restrictions of gender, class, and race in Marguerite Duras' novel, *The Lover*.[18] How could such a torrid love as this "fit" within the symbolics of early twentieth-century French or Indochinese culture? To speak such madness is to unleash "powers of horror" within the social symbolics of a dominant culture, but powers that open up new possibilities for engaging the "stranger" within and among us.

In summary, the third term of the ternary dispositions of embodied existence, offering itself as the originary site of poststructuralist philosophical and theological quests, is an eros of the remainders of symbolic systems. And as an eros of the limits, it does not seek to absorb or exterminate the "other" as the eros of binary thinking must do in order to keep the body "proper." Instead, operating at the threshold of the semiotic/symbolic dialectic, an eros of ternary existence terrifies the subject, tearing her/him from the stasis of normality, opening her/him to the plentitude of "bodily vision," culminating in excessive love for the "other." What then would theology be if it were to explore the terrain of such madness?

Theology as Somatology of "Wild Love"

In an article entitled "The End(s) of Theology," Mark C. Taylor says that theology since the early part of this century has wavered between emphasizing divine transcendence and divine immanence. The examples he gives for these extremes are Karl Barth, who affirmed divine transcendence to the denigration of all human achievement, and Thomas Altizer, who proposed a type of divine immanence in affirmation of the ultimate value of the earth. In response to both projects, Taylor writes:

> What have Barth and Altizer not thought? What does the alternative of transcendence and immanence leave out? Is there a nondialectical third that lies between the dialectic of either/or and both/and? Might this third be neither transcendent nor immanent? Does this neither/nor open the time-space of a different difference and another other—a difference and an other that do not merely invert but actually subvert the polarities of Western philosophical and theological reflection?[19]

For Taylor, the answer to these questions is a mode of writing which keeps us "open to a difference we cannot control and an other we can never master."[20] This is a writing of the limits, a parapraxis that resists the closure and nihilism of both a mode of religiosity which denigrates the world, and one which sanctifies it. Neither the "nay-saying" of neo-orthodox belief nor the "yea-saying" of secularized religion creates a space in which the sacred can be glimpsed—an affirmation of otherness and difference without "end."

While acknowledging differences of style and focus between Taylor's "a/theology" and the "somatology" developed in this study, I would like to use the framework of his critique for locating this project of transgressive corporeality within the spectrum of other contemporary theological projects. For his critique of modern forms of nay-saying and yea-saying as simple reversals of each other helps distinguish this project from other kinds of theology operating in our cultural setting today.

As suggested by Taylor, the nay-sayers of theology are all those projects which espouse transcendent entities or principles that are immune to critical review and function to denigrate the intrinsic value of human potential and achievement. As noted above, his primary example of nay-saying is the neo-orthodox Christianity of Karl Barth, with its proclamation of the utter otherness of the divine, an otherness that depicts human achievement as not only inferior but actually anti-God in its pretensions for truth. Nay-sayers in this schema are the prophets of revealed religion who call forth divine judgment on all those who "work out their own salvation" in the here and now. Nineteenth and early twentieth–century liberal theology is their primary target.

In applying this paradigm of nay-saying to the problematic of transgressive corporeality presented in this study, I begin with critiques that have become somewhat common in the current field of theological discourse. This first group of nay-sayers has many features of the old monk Jorge of Eco's novel. They are those guardians of transcendent truths from Tertullian to twentieth-century spokesmen of orthodoxy and neo-orthodoxy, who protect God from the encroachments of those who would in any way confuse or confound human thought and feeling with that of the divine. Revealed religion for these theorists must be untainted by the paradoxes and confusions of historical existence. And, as shown in Eco's novel, the protection of such "pure" truth carries a high price tag, that is, nothing less than the domestication or extermination of people and ideas identified with the margins.

But the nay-sayers of this somatology are not limited to the protectors of pristine religious truths. For even though a Barthian form of nay-saying excludes theologies which put too much reliance on human reason, there is another form of nay-saying which includes them. In an interesting twist of categories, in many manifestations of orthodoxy throughout Western history, reason (either alongside of revelatory truth or in place of it) has itself been elevated to the status of transcendent principle and thereby gone beyond the reaches of human evaluation or critique. Thus, the nay-sayers of this somatology include those voices of Western theology which have made reason so superior to feeling and culture so superior to nature that feeling and nature have become intrinsically inferior and thereby valuable only to the extent that they serve the needs and desires of the "civilized" world.

From the onset of Platonism in ancient Greece to the Jewish and Christian versions of middle and neo-Platonism in the early centuries of the Common Era to the Aristotelian scholasticism of medieval Europe to the Deism of the Enlightenment to the rationalism of the nineteenth century to the linguistic positivism of today, the priority of reason over the intuitions and passions of human life continues. And although this form of nay-saying may be less overtly oppressive than the nay-saying of theologies based on revelation, the effects of "rational" religiosity are not necessarily less dangerous. For when reason itself becomes a transcendental signified, then those people or structures of human life which are identified with reason become immune to criticism and constructive change. And that which appears the most benign and even beneficial to human life may in actuality be the most destructive. In the words of Foucault, the "body" in this Modern era has become imprisoned in an irrefutable "soul."

Although these nay-sayers have been, for the most part, repressive and controlling of bodily passions and of body identified people, the mechanisms of control have varied widely. As set forth cogently and convincingly by feminist theologians like Rosemary Ruether, Judith Plaskow, and Mary Daly, the most dangerous nay-sayers of religion are not the more overt mysogynists and body despisers but the more covert ones, those disguised as benign and rational representatives of the divine. Akin to the changes in discipline and punishment of the Modern era set forth by Foucault, the nay-sayers of Western religion have gone through various mutations. From the outright asceticism and cruelties of the medieval period reflected in the animosities and prejudices of Jorge, nay-sayers in the Enlightenment were transformed first into puritanical reformers and then into the supervisors of a religious orthodoxy which privileges male, Euro-American, heterosexuals. The present proponents of "family values" in American religion and politics are a prime contemporary example of such nay-saying.

These nay-sayers, it is important to note, are not simply misguided individuals but codes of culture internalized in people through the institutions and communication systems of postindustrial society. Whether locating immutable truths in propositions of a sacred text or in revelations of special experiences or in proofs of an irrefutable reason, these nay-sayers set up pyramids of power whereby the lower strata of their social structures are used to secure the privileges of those in the higher ones. Thus, the beliefs of these nay-sayers are in actuality mystifications of domination, hiding oppressive relations of exchange under the guise of transcendent truths. As witnessed by those at the bottom of such structures, these modes of theology not only fail to be salvific to those victimized by the system, they also erect barriers to salvation for the perpetrators. Their purported solutions are at least as damaging to the welfare of the earth as the problems they so desperately deplore.[21]

So the nay-sayers of Western theologies are anti-body in a binary economy which juxtaposes transcendence to immanence and reason to feeling, and denigrates the earth as the evil or sinful counterpart of salvific revelatory or rational realities. But while these nay-sayers of theology have elicited extensive study and critique in recent years by all but the most conservative voices in contemporary theology, the yea-sayers have been left largely unexamined and at times unwittingly condoned.

Who then are the yea-sayers? And how does their affirmation of the earth repeat the ill effects of their nay-saying counterparts? Again, initially following Taylor's lead, we turn to an analysis of theologies of immanence. But while Taylor's yea-sayers are descendents of Hegelian idealism who equate the divine with structures and achievements of human culture, the yea-sayers of this somatology are those who embrace the natural processes and entities of the earth as unequivocally good. Through an uncritical affirmation of the sacredness of the earth and of the body, yea-sayers retain a culture/nature dualism which makes nature an autonomous, self-justifying entity, immune to the critique of an "other" perspective. Thus, while the secular theologies of postwar American thought are the primary example of yea-saying for Taylor, the yea-sayers of this somatology extend beyond that.

Perhaps the best way to characterize the yea-sayers of this study is through their appropriation of the theory of a repressed natural goodness. The body for these theologies is a reservoir of feeling, spontaneity, and creativity that has been suppressed by dominant modes of culture. For the yea-sayers of certain kinds of feminist theology, this body is identified with women's history and experience. For some African-American theologies, it is identified with African-American history and experience. And for certain kinds of Native American, gay, lesbian, or womanist theologies, it is identified with their respective histories and experiences.

In summary, for all theologies which operate out of a theory of repressed natural goodness, their own particular experience and perspective becomes so identified with "natural truth" that it is immune to outside critique. A somatological yea-saying simply identifies the good with the repressed underside of a dominant cultural order rather than the order itself, and thereby creates yet another form of a transcendental signified immune to the critique of an other perspective. In the judgment of this study, any self-justifying perspective, whether tied to things above the earth or things upon it, has the same effect. It establishes a binary system of good and evil, and directs its negativity toward any who would confuse the two. The "will-to-truth" of a theology affirming divine immanence, therefore, can have just as much damaging force and fury as that of theologies insisting on divine transcendence. For in their sanctification of the earth, or anything identified with it, there is an implicit intolerance for that which calls this unmitigated good into question. And in this intolerance, the yea-sayers also do violence to those dwelling on the margins.

But here again, there is an ironic twist in the types of yea-saying emerging in our culture today. While the primary mode of a somatological yea-saying affirms natural impulses and feelings as the "real," another mode of yea-saying, erupting with a vengeance among our youth, is one that embraces the body as image, and calls for its uninhibited expression. This is a body of the simulacrum, exemplified in American culture by the antics of performers like Madonna. By mocking the traditional meaning of the symbols of Catholicism, and reducing these symbols to vehicles for the evocation of sexual feelings, Madonna creates a religion of the simulacrum, one which revels in the demise of all traditional religious truths without replacing those truths with anything of ethical import or substance.

But while Madonna and her pack of playful jesters are quickly condemned by the "serious" proponents of the Religious Right, the latter fail to recognize their own affinity with this kind of masquerade. For despite their publicly promoted puritanical sex codes, the Jimmy Bakers of commercialized religion in America are implicated in the same game as Madonna. Theirs is a religion of the simulacrum, a religiosity based solely on the evocative power of the image, and one which carries within it some of the same racist, sexist, and utilitarian values as its secular counterparts. Fundamentalist manipulators of the image are just as destructive to healthy body relations as those anti-religious performers whom they so heartily denounce.

But from naive earth lovers to hawkers of sexual images to preachers engaged in the commodification of religion, yea-sayers are as dangerous as their nay-saying counterparts. What makes them so? Kristeva's analysis of the dynamic of "mother love" within the writing of the Fascist writer Celine discloses the potential horror of this kind of affirmation of the body. For within a binary economy of good and evil, nature and the body are here seen as the good repressed underside of a bad cultural order. When such semiotic powers are appealed to as the indisputable "good" that needs simply to be released into culture to bring about the perfect society, then these powers have the potential to decimate the order which exists without providing a better alternative.

To put this into Foucault's terminology, if the "subjugated knowledges" of a cultural order are regarded as a self-justifying good, then they themselves become demonic as they overturn the dominant order and set themselves up as truth. In a binary economy of order versus disorder or dominant power/ knowledges versus subjugated ones, a simple reversal of power not only fails to solve the social/political problems that it sets out to solve, it can also set loose a whirlwind that destroys everything in its path, including its well-meaning but naive perpetrators.[22]

Thus, for a theology of embodied existence from a post-structuralist perspective, the source of theological thinking is neither the transcendent truths of revealed or rational religion nor the natural goodness of body-related groups or entities associated with the earth. Instead, it is the limits or margins of existence which call for reflection. And these margins, although by definition "unspeakable" within the symbolic codes of culture, nevertheless are critical for any theology which tries to break out of the confines of binary modes of thinking and being. Given the foray of Merleau-Ponty, Foucault, and Kristeva into the "margins" of poststructuralist aesthetics, how does this terrain of the margins relate to the theological task, and particularly to the role of religious symbols and rituals?

In Paul Tillich's articulation of a "theology of culture," he critiqued theologies that relied on the texts and rituals of a particular religious tradition for the questions which motivated their reflection. For Tillich, a myopic attention to the archives of one's own tradition is unresponsive to the issues of the wider culture. Thus, his coinage of the term, "theology of culture," was an attempt to broaden the base and source for questions which needed to be addressed by theologians. And these questions were most poignantly brought to our attention by artists. It was works of art, such as Picasso's "Guernica," which most powerfully raised the existential issues of political, social, and personal import that called for critical review and interpretation in Tillich's theology.[23]

The theology of the margins presented here, called by Carl Raschke "a somatology of the sensate markings we call culture," follows Tillich's lead in looking to a creative dynamic within contemporary culture as its "originating ground" for reflection. While the stories and symbols of a religious tradition do of course have importance for theology, they are not in themselves the source of theological investigation. Instead, it is the cross currents and tensions of everyday life that spawn the questions which need to be addressed in this enterprise called theology.

In addition, like Tillich's "theology of culture," a theology of the margins sees the aesthetic dimension of contemporary culture as the site where the questions of culture emerge with seductive force. But this dimension goes far beyond the works of art sitting in protective spaces in museums and performed for select audiences in symphony halls. In fact, the aesthetic is not a work of art at all, but the "sensate markings" or practices of culture operating in the "in-between" of everyday life. It is the graffiti of subway stations, the design of public spaces and buildings, the rhymes of children playing hopscotch, the jokes shared at the coffee pot. It is black leather jackets and pierced eyebrows—a whole realm of markings which we tend to pass by in our workday lives as we focus on other things. But at the edges of our vision, they persist. And through the lure of the dance of color, scent, texture and form, these markings at the edge of our awareness reveal the dynamic of cultural meanings in various stages of formation and deformation. It is the "sensate markings" of our lives which seduce us out of the ruts of habituated thinking and being. And it is only in awareness of and response to these markings that the enterprise of a theology of transgressive corporeality is fostered.

So a theology of the margins expands Tillich's arena of

questions that demand the attention of the theologian. In addition, it provides clues for answers to these questions. In a theology built upon firm foundations, one must discover answers to the questions of existence in the immutable features of one's own religious tradition. For some, this endeavor is achieved through the purported inerrancy of sacred texts. For others, it is through the evidence of foundational experiences. For still others, it is through the authority of the institution, the classics of the tradition, the fervour of emotions, or the universal values of rational people. Whatever the foundation may be, it provides the security of answers that are true, that is, immune to further critique and review.

Paul Tillich, for all his insight into the originating field of theological reflection, also looked for final answers to the existential questions of culture in his own religious tradition of Christianity. And although his answers are more sophisticated than those of a more conservative religious persuasion, they too are part of a foundationalist metaphysic in their claim to be the truth for all people. For Tillich, the answers of the Christian tradition are in fact superior to those of other religious traditions because of their ability to point to the truth of a "new reality" in a way that others cannot.[24]

In contrast to that kind of answer, the answers available within the "sensate markings" of this somatology are neither universal nor absolute. Yet, they are answers. They are answers in the way this theological quest broadens and deepens an understanding of one's cultural situation. That is, when a theologian of transgressive corporeality "reads" the sensate markings of culture, she/he sees more clearly which "will-to-truth" is operating in that setting, which practices are offering resistance, and, most important, where the possibilities of loving catharsis might be. The answers of this theology are more modes of insight into the dynamic of cultural meanings-in-process than irrefutable propositions.

In setting forth the components of a theology of transgressive corporeality, we began by placing this theology under the rubric of a "theology of culture," and then proceeded to compare this theology to that of Tillich's. In doing so, the notion of culture itself was expanded. For culture as presented by the three theorists of this study is neither the realm of the secular over against that of the sacred, nor the realm of human artifice and manipulation over against that of nature and the real.

Instead, the concept of culture developed here resists the dualism of binary thinking through its identification with a field of embodied relations traversed by forces of competing power/ knowledges. The sensate markings of this field are those wounds or remainders of body relations which mark the site of tension between dominant modes of power/knowledge and various modes of resistance. And a theology of transgressive corporeality is provoked into reflection by the intrusion into consciousness of these markings.

Underlying the articulation of this type of "theology of culture" is a kind of metaphysic—not foundational—which assures us of the continuation of the dynamic that is under investigation in this enterprise. At the beginning of chapter 2 of this study, we spoke of Nietzsche's legacy of unmasking as not only an unmasking of traditional or foundational modes of metaphysics, but also an "unmasking of unmasking." We called this a critique of "any stable structure of Being that governs becoming and gives meaning to knowledge and norms to conduct."[25] Throughout our examination of Merleau-Ponty's early work, we heard the specifics of his critique of this mode of metaphysics.

But then in an exploration of Merleau-Ponty's later work, we came across a concept of Being that was not a stable structure but rather a kind of "eternal recurrence." Sometimes Merleau-Ponty referred to this dynamic as elemental forces which prompt an upsurge of waves of expression in existence.[26] Sometimes he referred to it as the forces of "brute" or "wild Being" traversing the "flesh" of the world. At one time, he even spoke of it as the "phantom" which seduces the artist to creative expression. In each case, this Being was neither a "massive individual" external to the world, nor a stable structure within it. Instead, "wild Being" is a limit concept, the "inalienable horizon" within which we live our lives. And this horizon, through a "dehiscence of Being" makes possible all the rich variety of "visibles" in the world. Thus, for Merleau-Ponty, metaphysics does not need to be foundational in order to point to an "eternal recurrence" or dynamic within the processes of the world which has no beginning and, as far as we know, no end, and which provides the impetus for creative expression and relationship. "Wild Being," emanating out of the gap of human relations continually animates the "flesh" of the world.

But while Merleau-Ponty's "wild Being" decenters the self through wonder, it was not until our investigation of Foucault that we encountered another feature of this alternative metaphysic—relating such "Being" not only to the mystery but also to the madness of human existence. "Wild Being" for Foucault is a tiger, a wild animal untamed and untameable by our compulsive efforts for representation and control. Influenced by the work of Deleuze, Foucault in one place depicted this as a metaphysic of the "event." In contrast to a metaphysic of substance or coherence, a metaphysic of the event is not based on a unifying force but on "the recurrence of difference."[27] That is, instead of assuring us of some ultimate unity that underlies the variety and frictions of the world, a metaphysic of the event assures us that all unities are secondary to and dependent upon a prior crossing of forces that give rise to different kinds of order in different times and places. Given that all order is utilitarian in its processes and exclusionary in its results, a metaphysic of the event assures us of the "recurrence of difference" which disturbs and disrupts such order.[28] As the "wild Being" of madness rather than mystery, this mode of difference is one that can be frightening in its decentering of the self, and for Foucault, not always redemptive.

In continuing our exploration of an alternative metaphysic through the writings of Julia Kristeva, the effort was made to discriminate between a kind of madness which destroys and one which is life enhancing. And the contribution of Kristeva to this concept of "wild Being" is its identification with a healthy formation of selfhood spawned by relations of "wild love." For Kristeva, as discussed earlier, "wild love" is not the liberation of the repressed underside of cultural codes—an unmitigated release of the semiotic into the symbolic—but rather a catharsis of the boundary between the semiotic and symbolic which is ignited by co-creative relationships. "Wild love" then is not simply the "eternal recurrence of difference," but the neverending possibility of differences that give rise to an enhancement and revitalization of the "other." In this way, the "wild Being" of Merleau-Ponty and Foucault combine to draw our attention to a dynamic in the phenomenal world, which, although always decentering and often frightening, is the fertile field of life and growth for all bodies of the earth.[29]

A theology of transgressive corporeality is a "theology of culture" which is informed through one's peripheral vision of the limits of cultural practices. And the "sensate markings" or "remainders" of these limits, through their disturbance and disruption of patterns of normality, are the source of regeneration and growth. What then is the role of religious language in this theological model? And furthermore, how do the "margins" of theologies of liberation fit with the "limits" of a theology of transgressive corporeality?

It is probably evident to most people that religious stories and symbols are not necessarily true simply by virtue of being part of a religion. Furthermore, according to the concept of truth developed in this study, the truth or falsehood of religious symbols does not lie in their correspondence to realities outside the phenomenal world but to their performative effects within cultural practices. Religious language, then, is included within the other sensate markings of culture. It is part of the imaginary which creates a self through processes of displacement and decentering.

Yet religious language is not simply an optional substitute for other forms of cultural expression. Like other sensate markings of culture, religious stories and symbols arise out of the interactions of people in that culture. Like other markings, religious language is fluid in its import and meaning. In addition, it is true to the extent that it arises out of and gives voice to practices of ex-centric eros within a particular cultural setting. But the difference between other cultural poststructuralist aesthetics and religious poststructuralist aesthetics is the rootedness of the latter in an ongoing community shaping its identity through an intentional exploration of and reflection upon matters of ultimate concern.

Religious language, then, is important because of its location within and empowerment of a community of faith. And instead of being a catalyst for a catharsis of eros for individuals who may or may not be in community with others, religious language is rooted in communal experience, and fed through the regular performance of religious rituals. Although religious language may not differ in style from other sensate markings of culture, the conditions for its emergence and continuation are distinct. And these conditions are the practices of a community, which when acting "truthfully" are responsive to the cries of the limits. The language of communities of faith putting into practice an "eros" of the limits empowers healthy human subjectivity in a way that language shaping people in more isolated settings cannot achieve.

This brings us to our final question regarding the relationship of a theology of transgressive corporeality to theologies of liberation. More specifically, what is the relationship between the sensual remainders of the boundary between the symbolic and semiotic, and people who are socially and politically at the margins of dominant culture?

Returning to our analysis of binary structures, the "ontology of relatedness" of the dominant to subjugated groups in contemporary culture functions according to the Hegelian dialectic of master/slave relations. That is, the "master" and the "slave," although situated in quite different positions of power, nevertheless both operate out of the same ethic. Each uses the other for securing his/her own identity and possible advantage. When the marginalized of a culture speak out of the underside of this dialectic, without calling into question the dialectical structure itself, they are not speaking from the scene of abjection and of the "mother's desire." Instead, they are merely perpetuating the dialectic of a culture which oppresses them, trying to change from a position of the disadvantaged to that of privilege, and in so doing, condemning some "other" to victimization and domination.

If religious communities are to be truly responsive to the cry of the limits, they need to be at the margins of dominant codes of normality, but as argued in this study, the voices of the margins are not simply those of the disempowered or "subjugated knowledges" of cultures operating out of the binarism of mono-logical systems and structures. For as evidenced in Foucault's study of power/knowledge, such "subjugated knowledges" may simply be seeking dominance in a continuing war against the "other." In the field of theological reflection, these marginalized groups can be operating out of a nay-saying or a yea-saying. The first leans toward a foundationalism girded in the self-justifying truth of one's own tradition or thought. The second reduces theology to sociology, closing out the cries of the sacred through a reductionistic mode of secular humanism or claim to "pure" experience.

The sensate markings of the limit depicted here are not the repressed forces, psychic or social, of a "will-to-truth" operating within a binary economy of representation and domination. Rather, they are sites for the cathartic outbursts of eros radically calling into question and subverting the binary structure upon which systems of oppression operate and thereby mitigating the violence of reigning systems of signification as well as that of their suppressed counterparts. This outburst of eros, sparked by the "corp-o-sant" of "wild Being," emerges within the field of relationality and releases from out of its depths an aesthetics of cocreative relations. To trespass these margins is to enter into the "wilds" of loving, resilient relations.

Communities of faith, responsive to the seductions of this spirit, are sites of loving catharsis. And the role of the theologian as an engaged participant within such communities is twofold. First, aware of the dangers of mono-logical truths set within the framework of binary thinking, the theologian's task is that of the demystification and dismantling of such truths. In the terminology of Foucault, this is the role of the local intellectual, exposing the "hegemonies of truth" operating within and upon that cultural setting. And as suggested by Nietzsche's style of writing, such processes of demystification, coming as they do from the margins of discourse are not so much rational forms of argumentation as indirect messages of humor, irony, and poetics. The primary task of the theologian is to expose the relations of exchange upon which edifices of truth, including religious truth, are built and upheld, and to do so through the vehicle of indirect communication—the language of stories, poetry, songs, rituals, and of playful humor.[30]

But this deconstructive task doesn't end with that of demystification. For included within this speaking or writing of "indirect" messages is the call of those sensual remainders released within this process. That is, if one part of the task of theology is a dismantling of oppressive and repressive truths, then the other part, never separate from the first, is the gathering of those remainders or sensate markings of culture, *not* for the construction of a new system, but for a glimpse of an aesthetics of existence spawned by the eros of cocreative relations. It is these remainders that set the architectonic of religious truths aflame, and it is these remainders that resist the violence and counterviolence of structures of binary oppositions to become themselves the "originary site" of a new theological imagination.

And so it is that at the "end" of theology, we begin again

with that "marvelous and terrifying body" of "un-author-ized transgression," moving restively at the threshold of language and ravishing our hearts with the confusions of a "blessed, loving madness." She calls us from the margins, and it is her call that is a difference which makes a difference in human life and thought, without beginning and without end. Sobeit. A(wo)man.

Notes

1. See Gordon D. Kaufman, *The Theological Imagination: Constructing the Concept of God* (Philadelphia: The Westminster Press, 1981).

2. Ibid., 270.

3. Two examples of this critical component of theologies of construction are Gordon Kaufman's critique of the image/concept of God's sovereignty in *Theology for a Nuclear Age* (Philadelphia: Westminster Press, 1985), and Sallie McFague's critique of the image/concept of God as Father in *Models of God: Theology for an Ecological, Nuclear Age* (Philadelphia: Fortress Press, 1987).

4. Friedrich Nietzsche, *The Birth of Tragedy and The Case of Wagner*, trans. Walter Kaufmann (New York: Vintage Books, 1967), 52.

5. Note that just as the "masters of suspicion" historicized and radicalized Kant's conclusions on epistemology and ethics, so too Kant's aesthetics undergoes transformations in the hands of phenomenologists and poststructuralists. In contrast to the notion of beauty developed by Kant, the sublime deals with a mode of aesthetics that cannot be totalized or subsumed under a concept of unity.

6. Although these eras follow each other temporally, they are not necessarily tied to fixed time periods. Instead, they depict particular sets of epistemic relations.

7. Jacques Lacan, *Ecrits: A Selection*, trans. Alan Sheridan (New York: W. W. Norton, 1977), 2–24.

8. George Lindbeck in *The Nature of Doctrine* tends to define the theological enterprise along confessional lines, while Gordon Kaufman in *The Theological Imagination* and Sallie McFague in *Models of God* call for the evaluative critique of a wider public.

9. The danger of constructing a theology which replaces "traditional" symbols with "politically correct" ones is mitigated by an insistence on theology as a public enterprise. In *The Body of God: An Ecological Theology* (Minneapolis, Minnesota: Fortress, 1993), Sallie McFague insists that all theological models be judged according to their "commensurability with postmodern science as well as our own embodied experience and the well-being of the planet." (p. 149) Likewise, in *In Face of Mystery: a Constructive Theology* (Cambridge, Massachusetts: Harvard University Press, 1993), Gordon Kaufman appeals to a process of "reflective consciousness" which is constantly engaged in criticizing and reconstructing the dominant symbols of religion without ever attempting to "overcome and control the mystery within which we live." (p. 57). These qualifications show a sensitivity to the dangers of a theological pragmatism that can easily slide into a panopticism.

10. Merleau-Ponty, *The Visible and the Invisible*, 107.

11. Foucault, *The Order of Things*, 326.

12. Kristeva, *Powers of Horror*.

13. Note that this idea of eros as reunification goes back to Aristophanes' myth of the androgyne in Plato's *Symposium*. This was the concept of "eros" used in Paul Tillich's theology, which from the perspective of this study, provided a needed corrective to Anders Nygren's denigration of eros and yet didn't go far enough. As indicated earlier, the eros explored here is closer to the "madness" of Plato's *Phaedrus* then to the reunification of the androgyne. See Paul Tillich, *Systematic Theology*, 3 vols. (Chicago: University of Chicago Press, 1951–63.) and Anders Nygren, *Agape and Eros* trans. Philip Watson (Philadelphia: Westminster Press, 1953).

14. A recent work which explores the ethical aspects of this mode of eros is Edith Wyschogrod's *Saints and Postmodernism: Revisioning Moral Philosophy* (Chicago, Illinois: Uni-

versity of Chicago Press, 1990). Note how this "eros" is put into play, not by the need of the self but by that of the other.

15. As suggested by Jere Surber of the University of Denver, these wounds are symbolized in the Christian tradition in part by the "stigmata" of medieval Catholic hagiography.

16. Adrienne Rich, *The Fact of a Doorframe: Poems Selected and New, 1950–1984* (New York: Norton, 1984), 165.

17. Paule Marshall, *The Chosen Place, the Timeless People* (New York: Vintage Contemporaries, 1969).

18. Marguerite Dures, *The Lover*, trans. Barbara Bray (New York: Harper and Row, 1985).

19. Mark C. Taylor, "The End(s)of Theology" in *Theology at the End of Modernity*, ed. Sheila Greeve Davaney (Philadelphia: Trinity Press International, 1991), 242.

20. Ibid., 248.

21. Aside from a wide spectrum of feminist theologies which alert us to the dangers of theological nay-saying in respect to the lives of women, this critique has been elaborated upon by theologians voicing concerns on behalf of other bodies of the earth. For example, James B. Nelson in *Body Theology* (Louisville, Kentucky: Westminster/John Knox Press, 1992) shows the relationship of anti-body attitudes to homophobia and a truncated, violent form of masculinity. Sallie McFague in *The Body of God* and Rosemary Radford Ruether in *Gaia and God: An Ecofeminist Theology of Earth Healing* (San Francisco, California: Harper San Francisco, 1992) show how these modes of nay-saying endanger the well-being of our ecological systems, thereby negatively impacting all the bodies of the earth.

22. Two examples of this are the French Revolution of the eighteenth century and the National Socialist movement of this century.

23. Paul Tillich, "Protestantism and Artistic Style" in *Theology of Culture* (New York: Oxford University Press, 1959), 68–75.

24. Tillich, *Theology of Culture*, 40.

25. See above, p. 38.

26. See above, p. 65.

27. See above, p. 110.

28. Note that this poststructuralist appraisal of order differs significantly from a process approach which depends upon an harmonic order as a real possibility within history. For poststructuralists, all order is by definition exclusionary and thereby detrimental to *some* entities of the earth.

29. Although the theorists presented in this study are focused on human life and growth, their analysis does not necessarily exclude the intrinsic value of other nonhuman bodies. Sallie McFague differs from these theorists in that she is working out of a perspective that is more closely identified with process rather than poststructuralist thought, and yet her work is a good corrective to the tendency of poststructuralists to ignore the suffering and needs of the nonhuman world.

30. The turn to novels, films, and other forms of poetics in recent feminist theology is an example of this deconstructive "demystification." See especially the writings of Carol Christ, Delores Williams, and Rita Nakashima Brock.

Selected Bibliography

Books

Abel, Elizabeth, ed. *Writing and Sexual Difference*. Chicago: University of Chicago, 1982.

Agger, Ben. *The Decline of Discourse: Reading, Writing, and Resistance in Postmodern Capitalism*. New York: Falmer Press, 1990.

Allen, Jeffner and Iris Marion Young, eds. *The Thinking Muse: Feminism and Modern French Philosophy*. Bloomington: Indiana University Press, 1989.

Altizer, Thomas J. J. *The Self-Embodiment of God*. New York: Harper and Row, 1977.

Bakhtin, Mikhail. *The Dialogic Imagination*. Translated by Caryl Emerson and Michael Holquist. Austin: University of Texas Press, 1981.

Bannet, Eve Tavor. *Structuralism and the Logic of Dissent*. Chicago: University of Illinois Press, 1989.

Bataille, George. *Visions of Excess: Selected Writings, 1927–1939*. Translated by Allan Stockl. Minneapolis: University of Minnesota Press, 1985.

Bennington, Geoffrey and Jacques Derrida. *Jacques Derrida*. Translated by Geoffrey Bennington. Chicago: University of Chicago Press, 1993.

Blanchot, Maurice. *The Unavowable Community*. Translated by Pierre Joris. Barrytown, N.Y.: Station Hill Press, 1988.

Bordo, Susan. *The Flight to Objectivity: Essays on Cartesianism and Culture*. Albany: State University of New York Press, 1987.

Borgmann, Albert. *Crossing the Postmodern Divide.* Chicago: University of Chicago Press, 1992.

Borradori, Giovanna, ed. *Recording Metaphysics: The New Italian Philosophy.* Evanston, Ill.: Northwestern University Press, 1988.

Brown, Delwin. *To Set At Liberty: Christian Faith and Human Freedom.* Maryknoll, N.Y.: Orbis Books, 1981.

Brown, Norman O. *Love's Body.* New York: Random House, 1966.

Butler, Judith. *Gender Trouble: Feminism and the Subversion of Identity.* New York: Routledge, Chapman and Hall, Inc., 1990.

Bynum, Caroline. *Fragmentation and Redemption.* Cambridge: Massachusetts Institute of Technology Press, 1991.

Camporesi, Piero. *The Incorruptible Flesh: Bodily Mutilation and Mortification in Religion and Folklore.* Translated by Tania Croft-Murray. New York: Cambridge University Press, 1988.

Caputo, Joseph. *Radical Hermeneutics.* Bloomington, Ind.: Indiana University Press, 1988.

Carroll, David. *Paraesthetics: Foucault, Lyotard, Derrida.* New York: Methuen, 1987.

Chopp, Rebecca S. *The Power to Speak: Feminism, Language, God.* New York: Crossroad, 1989.

Chodorow, Nancy. *The Reproduction of Mothering.* Berkeley: University of California Press, 1978.

Coletti, Theresa. *Naming the Rose: Eco, Medieval Signs, and Modern Theory.* Ithaca, N.Y.: Cornell University Press, 1988.

Cooley, Paula, Sharon A. Farmer, and Mary Ellen Ross, eds. *Embodied Love: Sensuality and Relationship as Feminist Values.* San Francisco: Harper and Row, 1987.

Coward, Rosalind, and John Ellis. *Language and Materialism.* London: Routledge and Kegan Paul, 1977.

Crownfield, David, ed. *Body/Text in Julia Kristeva: Religion,*

Women, and Psychoanalysis. Albany: State University of New York Press, 1992.

Culler, Jonathan. *On Deconstruction: Theory and Criticism after Structuralism.* Ithaca: Cornell University Press, 1982.

Dallery, Arleen B. and Charles E. Scott, eds. *The Question of the Other: Essays in Contemporary Continental Philosophy.* Albany: State University of New York Press, 1989.

Daly, Mary. *Beyond God the Father: Toward a Philosophy of Women's Liberation.* Boston: Beacon Press, 1973.

Davaney, Sheila Greeve, ed. *Theology at the End of Modernity.* Philadelphia: Trinity Press International, 1991.

de Beauvoir, Simone. *Le Deuxieme Sexe.* (The Second Sex). Vol. 1. Paris: Gallimard, 1949.

de Certeau, Michel. *Heterologies: Discourse on the Other.* Translated by Brian Massumi. Minneapolis: University of Minnesota Press, 1986.

Deleuze, Gilles. *Difference et repetition.* Paris: Presses Universitaires de France, 1968.

————. *Logique du sens.* Paris: Editions de minuit, 1969.

————. *Nietzsche and Philosophy.* Translated by H. Tomlinson. New York: Columbia University Press, 1983.

————. *A Thousand Plateaus: Capitalism and Schizophrenia.* Minneapolis: University of Minnesota Press, 1987.

———— and Felix Guattari. *Anti-Oedipus: Capitalism and Schizophrenia.* Translated by R. Hurley, M. Seem, and H. R. Lane. New York: Viking Press, 1977.

———— and Claire Parnet. *Dialogues.* Translated by Hugh Tomlinson and Barbara Habberjam. New York: Columbia University Press, 1987.

Derrida, Jacques. *Dissemination.* Translated by Barbara Johnson. Chicago: University of Chicago Press, 1981.

————. *L'Ecriture et la difference* (Writing and Difference). Paris: Editions du Seuil, 1967.

————. *Margins of Philosophy.* Translated by Alan Bass. Chicago: University of Chicago Press, 1982.

————. *Positions*. Translated by Alan Bass. Chicago: University of Chicago Press, 1981.

————. *Speech and Phenomena and Other Essays on Husserl's Theory of Signs*. Evanston, Ill.: Northwestern University Press, 1973.

Descombes, Vincent. *Modern French Philosophy*. Translated by L. Scott-Fox and J. M. Harding. New York: Cambridge University Press, 1980.

Diamond, Irene, and Lee Quinby, eds. *Feminism and Foucault: Reflections on Resistance*. Boston: Northeastern University Press, 1988.

Docherty, Thomas. *After Theory: Postmodernism/Postmarxism*. New York: Routledge, 1990.

Dreyfus, Hubert L. and Paul Rabinow, eds. *Michel Foucault: Beyond Structuralism and Hermeneutics*. Chicago: University of Chicago Press, 1982.

Duras, Marguerite. *The Lover*. Translated by Barbara Bray. New York: Harper and Row, 1985.

Eagleton, Terry. *Against the Grain: Essays 1975–1985*. London and New York: Verso, 1986.

————. *The Function of Criticism: From the Spectator to Post-Structuralism*. New York: Verso, 1984.

————. *The Ideology of the Aesthetic*. Cambridge, Mass.: Basil Blackwell Inc., 1990.

Eagleton, Terry, Frederick Jameson, and Edward W. Said. *Nationalism, Colonialism, and Literature*. Minneapolis: University of Minnesota Press, 1990.

Eco, Umberto. *The Name of the Rose*. Translated by William Weaver. New York: Harcourt, Brace, Jovanovich, 1983.

Eisenstein, Hester and Alice Jardine. *The Future of Difference*. New Brunswick, N.J.: Rutgers University Press, 1985.

Farley, Edward. *Good and Evil: Interpreting a Human Condition*. Minneapolis: Fortress Press, 1990.

Fischer, Michael. *Does Deconstruction Make Any Difference?*

Poststructuralism and the Defense of Poetry in Modern Criticism. Bloomington: Indiana University Press, 1985.

Flax, Jane. *Thinking Fragments: Psychoanalysis, Feminism, and Postmodernism in the Contemporary West.* Berkeley: University of California Press, 1990.

Fletcher, John and Andrew Benjamin, eds. *Abjection, Melancholia and Love: The Work of Julia Kristeva.* New York: Routledge, 1990.

Foucault, Michel. *Histoire de la folie e l'age classique.* (Madness and Civilisation: A History of Insanity in the Age of Reason.) Paris: Editions Gallimard, 1972.

———. *Language, Counter-memory, Practice: Selected Essays and Interviews.* Translated by Donald F. Bouchard and Sherry Simon. Edited by Donald F. Bouchard. Ithaca: Cornell University Press, 1977.

———. *Michel Foucault, Politics, Philosophy, Culture: Interviews and Other Writings, 1977–1984.* Edited by Lawrence D. Kritzman. New York: Routledge, Chapman and Hall, 1988.

———. *Moi, Pierre Riviere ayant egorge ma mere, ma soeuret-mon frere.* (I, Pierre Riviere, Having Slaughtered My Mother, My Sister, and My Brother: A Case of Parricide in the 19th Century.) Paris: Editions Gallimard, 1973.

———. *Les Mots et les Choses. Une archeologie des sciences humaines.* (The Order of Things: An Archaelogy of the Human Sciences.) Paris: Editions Gallimard, 1966.

———. *Naissance de la clinique. Une archeologie du reard medical.* (The Birth of the Clinic: An Archaeology of Medical Perception.) rev. ed. Paris: Editions Gallimard, 1972.

———. *Power/Knowledge: Selected Interviews and Other Writings 1972–1977.* Edited by Colin Gordon. New York: Pantheon Books, 1980.

———. *Le Souci de soi.* Vol. 3. *Historie de la sexualite.* (The History of Sexuality, Vol. 3: The Care of the Self.) Paris: Editions Gallimard, 1984.

———. *Surveiller et Punir. Naissance de la prison.* (Discipline

and Punish: Birth of the Prison.) Paris: Editions Gallimard, 1975.

——. *L'Usage des plaisirs.* Vol. 2. *Historie de le sexualite.*
(The History of Sexuality, Vol. 2: The Use of Pleasure.)
Paris: Editions Gallimard, 1984.

——. *La volente de savoir.* Vol. 1, *Historie de la sexualite.*
(The History of Sexuality, Vol. 1: An Introduction.) Paris:
Editions Gallimard, 1978.

——. *Michel Foucault, Politics, Philosophy, Culture: Interviews and Other Writings, 1977–1984.* Edited by Lawrence
D. Kritzman. New York: Routledge, Chapman and Hall,
1988.

Foucault, Michel, ed. *Herculine Barbin, dite Alexina B. pre-
sente par Michel Foucault.* (Herculine Barbin, Being the
Recently Discovered Memoirs of a Nineteenth-Century Her-
maphrodite.) Paris: Editions Gallimard, 1978.

Fraser, Nancy. *Unruly Practices: Power, Discourse and Gender in Contemporary Social Theory.* Minneapolis: University of Minnesota Press, 1989.

Fuss, Diana. *Essentially Speaking.* New York: Routledge,
Chapman, and Hall, 1989.

Gaines, Jane and Charlotte Herzog, eds. *Fabrications: Costume and the Female Body.* New York: Routledge, 1990.

Gallagher, Catherine and Thomas Laquer, eds. *The Making of
the Modern Body: Sexuality and Society in the Nineteenth
Century.* Berkeley: University of California Press, 1987.

Garner, Shirley, Claire Kahane, and Madelon Sprenger, eds.
The (M)Other Tongue. Ithaca: Cornell University Press,
1985.

Gasche, Rodolphe. *The Tain of the Mirror.* Cambridge, Mass.:
Harvard University Press, 1986.

Gates, Henry Louis, Jr. *"Race," Writing, and Difference.* Chicago: University of Chicago Press, 1986.

Gelfand, Elissa D. and Virginia Thorndike Hules. *French Feminist Criticism: Women, Language, Literature. An Anno-
tated Bibliography.* New York: Garland Publishing, 1985.

Giddons, Anthony. *The Consequences of Modernity*. Stanford: Stanford University Press, 1990.

Gilman, Sandra L. *Difference and Pathology: Stereotypes of Sexuality, Race and Madness*. Ithaca, N.Y.: Cornell University Press, 1985.

Girard, Rene. *Violence and the Sacred*. Translated by Patrick Gregory. Baltimore: Johns Hopkins University Press, 1977.

Graybeal, Jean. *Language and "the feminine" in Nietzsche and Heidegger*. Bloomington: Indiana University Press, 1990.

Haddon, Genie Pauli. *Body Metaphors: Releasing God-feminine in Us All*. New York: Crossroad, 1988.

Harraway, Donna J. *Simians, Cyborgs, and Women: The Reinvention of Nature*. New York: Routledge, 1991.

Hegel, G. W. F. *Phenomenology of Spirit*. Translated by A. V. Miller. New York: Oxford University Press, 1977.

Heidegger, Martin. *The Question Concerning Technology and Other Essays*. Translated by William Lovitt. New York: Harper and Row, 1977.

———. *What is Called Thinking?*. Translated by J. Glenn Gray. New York: Harper and Row, 1968.

Hekman, Susan J. *Gender and Knowledge: Elements of a Postmodern Feminism*. Boston: Northeastern University Press, 1990.

Henriques, Julian. *Changing the Subject: Psychology, Social Regulation and Subjectivity*. New York: Methuen, 1984.

Heyward, Carter. *Touching Our Strength: The Erotic as Power and the Love of God*. San Francisco: Harper and Row, 1989.

Hutcheon, Linda. *A Poetics of Postmodernism: History, Theory, Fiction*. New York: Routledge, 1988.

Irigaray, Luce. *Marine Lover of Friedrich Nietzsche*. Translated by Gillian C. Gill. New York: Columbia University Press, 1991.

————. *Ce sexe qui n'en est pas un.* (This Sex Which is Not One.) Paris: Editions de Minuit, 1977.

————. *Speculum of the Other Woman.* Translated by Gillian C. Gill. Ithaca: Cornell University Press, 1985.

Jacobus, Mary. *Reading Woman: Essays in Feminist Criticism.* New York: Columbia University Press, 1986.

Jaggar, Alison M., and Susan Bordo, eds., *Gender/Body/Knowledge.* New Brunswick: Rutgers University Press, 1989.

Johnson, Galen A. and Michael B. Smith, eds. *Ontology and Alterity in Merleau-Ponty.* Evanston, Ill.: Northwestern University Press, 1990.

Kaufman, Gordon. *In Face of Mystery: A Constructive Theology.* Cambridge, Mass.: Harvard University Press, 1993.

————. *The Theological Imagination: Constructing the Concept of God.* Philadelphia: Westminster Press, 1981.

————. *Theology for a Nuclear Age.* Philadelphia: Westminster Press, 1985.

Krell, David Farrell and David C. Wood, eds., *Exceedingly Nietzsche.* New York: Routledge, 1988.

Kristeva, Julia. *Black Sun: Depression and Melancholia.* Translated by Leon S. Roudiez. New York: Columbia University Press, 1989.

————. *Des Chinoises.* (About Chinese Women.) Paris: des femmes, 1974.

————. *Desire in Language: A Semiotic Approach to Literature and Art.* Translated by Alice Jardine, Thomas A. Gora and Leon S. Roudiez. Edited by Leon Roudiez. New York: Columbia University Press, 1980.

————. *Etranges a nous memes.* (Strangers to Ourselves.) Paris: Editions du Seuil, 1989.

————. *Histories d'amour.* Paris: Denoel, 1983.

————. *Polylogue.* Paris: Editions de Seuil, 1977.

————. *Pouvoirs de l'horreur.* (Powers of Horror: An Essay on Abjection.) Paris: Editions de Seuil, 1980.

————. *La Revolution du langage poetique.* (Revolution in Poetic Language.) Paris: Editions du Seuil, 1974.

Lacan, Jacques. *Ecrits: A Selection.* Translated by Alan Sheridan. New York: W. W. Norton, 1977.

Lacquer, Thomas and Catherine Gallagher, eds. *The Making of the Modern Body: Sexuality and Society in the Nineteenth Century.* Berkeley: University of California Press, 1987.

Leder, Drew. *The Absent Body* Chicago: University of Chicago Press, 1990.

Levin, David Michael. *The Body's Recollection of Being: Phenomenological Psychology and the Deconstruction of Nihilism.* London: Routledge and Kegan Paul, 1985.

————. *The Opening of Vision: Nihilism and the Postmodern Situation.* London: Routledge, Chapman and Hall, 1988.

Lindbeck, George. *Nature of Doctrine: Religion and Theology in a Post-Liberal Age.* Philadelphia: Westminster Press, 1984.

Lingis, Alphonso. *Excesses: Eros and Culture.* Albany: State University of New York Press, 1983.

Lowe, Walter. *Evil and the Unconscious.* American Academy of Religion Studies in Religion No. 30. Chico, Calif.: Scholars Press, 1983.

Lyotard, Jean-Francois. *The Postmodern Condition: A Report on Knowledge.* Minneapolis: University of Minnesota Press, 1984.

Macksey, Richard and Eugenio Donato, eds. *The Structuralist Controversy.* Baltimore: Johns Hopkins University Press, 1972.

Marcuse, Herbert. *Eros and Civilization: A Philosophical Inquiry Into Freud.* Boston: Beacon Press, 1966.

Marks, Elaine and Isabellede Courtivron, eds. *New French Feminisms: An Anthology.* New York: Schocken Books, 1980.

Marks, Elaine and George Stambolian, eds. *Homosexualities and French Literature: Cultural Contexts/Critical Texts.* Ithaca: Cornell University Press, 1979.

Marshall, Paule. *The Chosen Place, the Timeless People.* New York: Vintage Contemporaries, 1969.

Martin, Randy. *Performance as Political Act: The Embodied Self.* New York: Bergin and Garvey, 1990.

McFague, Sallie. *The Body of God: An Ecological Theology.* Minneapolis: Fortress Press, 1993.

———. *Metaphorical Theology: Models of God in Religious Language.* Philadelphia: Fortress Press, 1982.

———. *Models of God: Theology for an Ecological, Nuclear Age.* Philadelphia: Fortress Press, 1987.

McMillan, C. *Woman, Reason and Nature.* Princeton: Princeton University Press, 1982.

Megill, Allen. *Prophets of Extremity: Nietzsche, Heidegger, Foucault, Derrida.* Los Angeles: University of California Press, 1985.

Merleau-Ponty, Maurice. *Adventures of the Dialectic.* Translated by Joseph Bien. Evanston, Ill.: Northwestern University Press, 1973.

———. *Phenomenologie de la perception.* (Phenomenology of Perception). Paris: Presses Universitaires de France, 1946.

———. *The Prose of the World.* Translated by John O'Neill. Evanston, Ill.: Northwestern University Press, 1973.

———. *Le Visible et l'invisible.* (The Visible and the Invisible.) Paris: Gallimard, 1964.

———. *Signs.* Translated by Richard C. McCleary. Evanston, Ill.: Northwestern University Press, 1964.

Merchant, Carolyn. *The Death of Nature: Women, Ecology and the Scientific Revolution.* San Francisco: Harper and Row, 1980.

Michie, Helena. *The Flesh Made Word: Female Figures and Women's Bodies.* New York: Oxford University Press, 1987.

Miles, Margaret R. *Carnal Knowing: Female Nakedness and Religious Meaning in the Christian West.* New York: Vintage Books, 1991.

Moi, Toril. *Sexual/Textual Politics: Feminist Literary Theory*. New York: Methuen, 1985.

———. *The Kristeva Reader*. New York: Columbia University Press, 1986.

Montefiori, Alan, ed. *Philosophy in France Today*. New York: Cambridge University Press, 1983.

Mulvey, Laura. *Visual and Other Pleasures*. Bloomington, Ind.: Indiana University Press, 1989.

Murray, David, ed. *Forked Tongues: Speech, Writing, and Representation in North American Indian Texts*. Bloomington: Indiana University Press, 1991.

Nelson, James B. *Body Theology*. Louisville, Ky.: Westminster/ John Knox Press, 1992.

———. *Embodiment: An Approach to Sexuality and Christian Theology*. Minneapolis: Augsburg Publishing House, 1978.

Nicholson, Linda J., ed. *Feminism/Postmodernism*. New York: Routledge, 1990.

Nietzsche, Friedrich. *The Gay Science*. Translated by Walter Kaufman. New York: Random House, 1974.

———. *The Birth of Tragedy and the Genealogy of Morals*. Translated by Francis Golffing. Garden City, N.Y.: Doubleday, 1956.

———. *Thus Spoke Zarathustra: a Book for All and None*. Translated by Walter Kaufman. New York: Viking Penguin Inc., 1966.

———. *The Will to Power*. Translated by Walter Kaufmann. New York: Random House, 1967.

Nye, Andrea. *Words of Power: A Feminist Reading of the History of Logic*. New York: Routledge, 1990.

Nygren, Anders. *Agape and Eros*. Translated by Philip Watson. Philadelphia: Westminster Press, 1953.

Pefanis, Julian. *Heterology and the Postmodern: Bataille, Baudrillard, and Lyotard*. Durham, N.C.: Duke University Press, 1991.

Polhemus, Robert M. *Erotic Faith: Being in Love from Jane Austen to D. H. Lawrence.* Chicago: University of Chicago Press, 1990.

Raschke, Carl A. *The Alchemy of the Word: Language and the End of Theology.* Missoula, Montana: Scholars Press, 1979.

————. *Painted Black: From Drug Killings to Heavy Metal—the Alarming True Story of How Satanism is Terrorizing Our Communities.* New York: Harper and Row, 1990.

————. *Theological Thinking: An In-quiry.* Atlanta: Scholars Press, 1988.

Rich, Adrienne. *The Fact of a Doorframe: Poems Selected and New, 1950–1984.* New York: Norton, 1984.

Ricoeur, Paul. *Hermeneutics and the Human Sciences: Essays on Language, Action, and Interpretation.* Cambridge: Cambridge University Press, 1981.

————. *Oneself as Another.* Translated by Kathleen Blamey. Chicago: University of Chicago Press, 1992.

Rorty, Richard. *Philosophy and the Mirror of Nature.* Princeton, N.J.: Princeton University Press, 1978.

Rose, Jacqueline. *Sexuality in the Field of Vision.* London: Verso, 1987.

Ruether, Rosemary Radford. *Gaia and God: An Ecofeminist Theology of Earth Healing.* San Francisco: Harper San Francisco, 1992.

Scarry, Elaine. *The Body in Pain: The Making and Unmaking of the World.* Oxford: Oxford University Press, 1986.

Scharlemann, Robert, ed. *Deconstruction and Theology.* New York: Crossroads, 1982.

Scott, Charles E. *The Language of Difference.* Atlantic Highlands, N.J.: Humanities Press International, Inc., 1987.

Sebeok, Thomas, ed. *The Tell-Tale Sign: A Survey of Semiotics.* Lisse, Belgium: The Peter de Ridder Press, 1975.

Shafer, Ingrid, ed. *The Incarnate Imagination: Essays in*

Theology, the Arts and Social Sciences. Bowling Green, Ohio: Bowling Green State University Press, 1988.

Silverman, Hugh and Gary E. Aylesworth, eds. *The Textual Sublime: Deconstruction and Its Differences.* Albany, N.Y.: State University of New York, 1990.

Silverman, Kaja. *The Acoustic Mirror: The Female Voice in Psychoanalysis and Literature.* Bloomington: Indiana University Press, 1988.

Smith, Steven. *The Argument to the Other.* Chico, Calif.: Scholars Press, 1983.

Spivak, Gayatri Chakravorty. *In Other Worlds: Essays in Cultural Politics.* New York: Routledge, 1988.

Suleiman, Susan Rubin, ed. *The Female Body in Western Culture.* Cambridge: Harvard University Press, 1986.

Taylor, Mark C. *Altarity.* Chicago: University of Chicago Press, 1987.

———. *Deconstructing Theology.* American Academy of Religion Studies in Religion No. 28. Chico, Calif.: Scholars Press, 1982.

———. *Deconstruction in Context: Literature and Philosophy.* Chicago: University of Chicago Press, 1986.

———. *Disfiguring: Art, Architecture, Religion.* Chicago: University of Chicago Press, 1992.

———. *Erring: A Postmodern A/theology.* Chicago: University of Chicago Press, 1984.

———. *Journeys to Selfhood: Hegel and Kierkegaard.* Berkeley: University of California Press, 1981.

———. *Nots.* Chicago: University of Chicago Press, 1993.

Tillich, Paul. *Systematic Theology.* 3 vols. Chicago: University of Chicago Press, 1951–63.

———. *Theology of Culture.* Edited by Robert C. Kimball. New York: Oxford University Press, 1959.

Tracy, David. *The Analogical Imagination: Christian Theology and the Culture of Pluralism.* New York: Crossroads, 1981.

Tyler, Stephen A. *The Unspeakable: Discourse, Dialogue, and Rhetoric in the Postmodern World.* Madison: University of Wisconsin Press, 1987.

Vance, Carol, ed. *Pleasure and Danger.* Boston: Routledge, 1984.

Welch, Sharon. *Communities of Resistance and Solidarity: a Feminist Theology of Liberation.* Maryknoll, N.Y.: Orbis, 1985.

————. *A Feminist Ethic of Risk.* Minneapolis: Fortress Press, 1990.

Winquist, Charles E. *Epiphanies of Darkness: Deconstruction in Theology.* Philadelphia: Fortress Press, 1986.

Wood, David C. and Robert Bernasconi, eds. *Derrida and Difference.* Evanston, Ill.: Northwestern University Press, 1988.

Wyatt, Jean. *Reconstructing Desire: The Role of the Unconscious in Woman's Reading and Writing.* Chapel Hill, N.C.: University of North Carolina Press, 1990.

Wyschogrod, Edith. *Saints and Postmodernism: Revisioning Moral Philosophy.* Chicago: University of Chicago Press, 1990.

————. *Spirit in Ashes: Hegel, Heidegger and Man-Made Mass Death.* New Haven: Yale University Press, 1985.

Wyschogrod, Edith, David Crownfield and Carl A. Raschke, eds. *Lacan and Theological Discourse.* Introduction by David H. Fisher. Comments by David Crowndield. Albany, N.Y.: State University of New York Press, 1989.

Articles in Monographs

Abraham, Nicolas and Maria Torak. "Notes on the Phantom: A Complement to Freud's Metapsychology." In *The Trial(s) of Psychoanalysis,* ed. Francoise Meltzer. Chicago: University of Chicago Press, 1987:75–80.

Benhabid, Seyla. "The Generalized and the Concrete Other:

the Kohlberg-Gilligan Controversy and Moral Theory." In *Women and Moral Theory*, eds. Eva Kittay and Diana Meyers. Totowa, N.J.: Rowman and Littlefield Press, 1987:154–77.

Blonsky, Marshall. "The Agony of Semiotics: Reassessing the Discipline." In *On Signs*, ed. Marshall Blonsky. Baltimore: The John Hopkins University Press, 1985:xiii–ii.

Chopp, Rebecca S. "Feminist Theology as Political Theology: Visions on the Margins." In *Theology, Politics, and Peace*, ed. Theodore Runyon. Maryknoll, N.Y.: Orbis Books, 1989:148–58.

Jameson, Fredric. "Postmodernism and Consumer Society." In *The Anti-Aesthetic; Essays on Postmodern Culture*, ed. Hal Foster. Port Townsend, Wash.: Bay Press, 1983:47–59.

Jones, Ann Rosalind. "Inscribing Femininity: French Theories of the Feminine." In *Making a Difference*, eds. G. Greene and E. Kahn. London: Methuen, 1985:213–28.

———. "Writing the Body: Toward an Understanding of *l'Ecriture feminine*. In *The New Feminist Criticism: Essays on Women, Literature, and Theory*, ed. Elaine Showalter. New York: Pantheon Books, 1985:361–78.

Kittay, Eva Feder. "Pornography and the Erotics of Domination." In *Beyond Domination*, ed. Carol Gould. Totowa, N.Y.: Rowman and Allenheld, 1983:145–74.

Kristeva, Julia. "Postmodernism?" In *Romanticism, Modernism, Postmodernism*, ed. Harry Garvin. Lewisburg, Penn.: Bucknell University Press, 1980:136–41.

Ruether, Rosemary Radford. "Theologizing From the Side of the 'Other': Women, Blacks, Indians and Jews." In *Faith That Transforms: Essays in Honor of Gregory Baum*, eds. M. Leddy and M. Hinsdale. New York: Paulist Press, 1987:62–81.

Solle, Dorothee. "Between Matter and Spirit: Why and in What Sense Must Theology be Materialist?" In *God of the Lowly*, eds. W. Schottroft and W. Stegemann. Maryknoll, N.Y.: Orbis Books, 1984:86–102.

Spivak, Gayatri. "Displacement and the Discourse of Woman."

In *Displacement: Derrida and After*, ed. Mark Krupnick. Bloomington: Indiana University Press, 1983:88–102.

————. "Explanation and Culture: Marginalia." In *In Other Worlds: Essays in Cultural Politics*, ed. Mark Krupnick. New York: Routledge, 1987:110–24.

Taylor, Mark C. "Refusal of the bar." In *Lacan and Theological Discourse*, eds. Edith Wyschogrod, et. als. Albany, N.Y.: State University of New York, 1989:39–53.

Weigel, Sigrid. "Double Focus: on the History of Women's Writing." Translated by Harriet Anderson. In *Feminist Aesthetics*, ed. Gisela Ecker. London: Women's Press, 1985:43–56.

Welch, Sharon. "Ideology and Social Change." In *Weaving the Visions*, eds. Judith Plaskow and Carol Christ. San Francisco: Harper and Row, 1989:336–343.

Winquist, Charles E. "The Surface of the Deep: Deconstruction in the Study of Religion." In *The Whirlwind in Culture*, eds. Donald Musser and Joseph Price. Bloomington, Ind.: Meyer-Stone Books, 1988:55–66.

Dissertations

Altmann, Ronald Walter. "Being-in-the-World and Corporeality." Ph.D. diss., Duquesne University, 1981.

Bernal, Ellen Wells. "The Meaning of Embodiment in the Thought of Michael Polanyi and Maurice Merleau-Ponty." Ph.D. diss., Duke University, 1980.

Capuzzi, Frank Anthony. "The Ethics of the Body: Merleau-Ponty's Implicit Critique of Kant's Moral Philosophy." M.A. thesis, Duquesne University, 1970.

Mahon, Michael Gerard. "Foucault's Nietzschean Genealogy: a Study of Michel Foucault's Nietzschean Problematic, 1961–1975." Ph.D. diss., Boston College, 1989.

McWhorten, Donna Ladelle. "Theory and Beyond: Foucault's Relevance for Feminist Thinking." Ph.D. diss., Vanderbilt University, 1986.

Ray, Stephen. "The Modern Soul: Michel Foucault and the Theological Discourse of Gordon Kaufman and David Tracy." Ph.D. diss., Harvard University, 1986.

Spinello, Richard Arthur. "Nietzsche's Conception of the Body." Ph.D. diss., Fordham University, 1981.

Welch, Sharon Diane. "The Battle for Truth: Foucault, Liberation Theology and the Insurrection of Subjugated Knowledges." Ph.D. diss., Vanderbilt University, 1982.

Williams, Jay. "Toward a 'Bodily Hermeneutics': A Phenomenological Investigation of Primordial Intentionality and Meaning." Ph.D. diss., State University at Stoney Brook, 1984.

Yount, Mark. "Meaning in the Play of Difference: Between Hermeneutics and Deconstruction." Ph.D. diss., University of Colorado at Boulder, 1986.

Journal Articles

Bordo, Susan. "The Cartesian Masculinization of Thought." Signs 2 (Fall 1980): 439–56.

Brown, Delwin. "Struggle till Daybreak: On the Nature of Authority in Theology." The Journal of Religion 65 (January 1985): 15–32.

————. "Transforming Tradition: History, Creativity, and the Task of Theology." The Iliff Review 41 (Fall 1984): 3–15.

Chidester, David. "Michel Foucault and the Study of Religion." Religious Studies Review 12 (January 1986): 1–9.

Gilmour, John C. "Art and the Expression of Meaning." Process Studies 13 (Spring 1983): 71–87.

Heimonet, Jean-Michel. "From Bataille to Derrida: Differance and Heterology." Translated by A. Engstrom. Stanford French Review 12 (Spring 1988): 129–47.

Jardine, Alice. "Pre-Texts for the Transatlantic Feminist." Yale French Studies 62 (Spring 1981): 220–36.

————. "Theories of the Feminine: Kristeva." enclitic 4 (Autumn 1980): 5–15.

Jones, Ann Rosalind. "Julia Kristeva on Femininity: the Limits of a Semiotic Politics." *Feminist Review* 18 (November 1984): 56–73.

———. "Writing the Body: Toward an Understanding of L'Ecriture Feminine," *Feminist Studies* 7 (Summer 1981): 247–63.

Joy, Morny. "Derrida and Ricoeur: A Case of Mistaken Identity (and Difference)." *Journal of Religion* 68 (Fall 1988): 508–26.

Kisley, Lorraine. "The Body." *Parabola* 10 (Summer 1985): 6–73.

Kitagawa, Joseph M. "The Body." *History of Religions* 30 (August 1990): 1–102.

Miles, Margaret R. "Revisioning an Embodied Christianity." *Unitarian Universalist Christian* 42 (January 1987): 5–13.

Moore, Stephen. "The 'Post-' Age Stamp: Does It Stick?" *Journal of the American Academy of Religion* 57 (Fall 1989): 88–97.

Odin, Steve. "Blossom Scents Take Up the Ringing: Synaesthesia in Japanese and Western Aesthetics." *Soundings* 69 (Fall 1986): 256–81.

Ophir, Adi. "Michel Foucault and the Semiotics of the Phenomenal." *Dialogue* 23 (Spring 1988): 408–12.

Pellauer, David. "Embodiment and Philosophical-Theological Reflection." *Dialog* 27 (Summer 1988): 174–77.

Raschke, Carl. "The Deconstructive Imagination: a Response to Mark Taylor." *Religion and Intellectual Life* 5 (Winter 1988): 37–43.

———. "Fire and Roses: Toward Authentic Post-Modern Religious Thinking." *Journal of the American Academy of Religion* 58 (Winter 1990): 671–89.

———. "From Textuality to Scripture: the End of Theology as 'Writing.' " *Semeia* 40 (Summer 1987): 39–52.

Ross-Bryant, Lynn. "The Land in American Religious Experience." *Journal of the American Academy of Religion* 66 (January 1986): 37–45.

Salving, Valerie C. "Our Bodies/Our Selves: Reflections on Sickness, Aging, and Death." *Journal of Feminist Studies* 4 (Fall 1988): 117–25.

Shapiro, Susan E. "Failing Speech: Post-Holocaust Writing and the Discourse of Postmodernism." *Semia* 40 (Fall 1987): 65–91.

Sheridan, Daniel P. "Discerning Difference: a Taxonomy of Culture, Spirituality and Religion." *Journal of Religion* 66 (January 1986): 37–45.

Smith, Ruth L. "The Evasion of Otherness: a Problem for Feminist Moral Reconstruction." *Union Seminary Quarterly Review* 43 (Fall 1989): 145–61.

Spelman, Elizabeth V. "Woman as Body: Ancient and Contemporary Views." *Feminist Studies.* 8 (Spring 1982): 24–43.

Spivak, Gayatri Chakravorty. "French Feminism in an International Frame." *Yale French Studies* 62 (Spring 1987): 154–84.

Stout, Jeffrey. "A Lexicon of Postmodern Philosophy." *Religious Studies Review* 13 (Winter 1986): 18–22.

Taylor, Mark C. "Deconstruction: What's the Difference?" *Soundings* 66 (winter 1983): 401–2.

———. "Shades of Difference." *Semeia* 40 (Fall 1987): 21–38.

Thiemann, Ronald F. "Revelation and Imaginative Construction." *Journal of Religion* 61 (Fall 1981): 242–63.

Vanhoozer, Kevin J. "A Lamp in the Labyrinth: the Hermeneutics of 'Aesthetic' Theology." *Trinity Journal* 8 (Spring 1987): 25–56.

Welch, Sharon D. "A Genealogy of the Logic of Deterrence: Haberman, Foucault and a Feminist Ethic of Risk." *Union Seminary Quarterly Review* 41 (Winter 1987): 13–32.

Winquist, Charles. "The Epistemology of Darkness: Preliminary Reflections." *Journal of the American Academy of Religion* 49 (Winter 1981): 24–43.

————. "Theology, Deconstruction, and Ritual Process." *Zygon: Journal of Religion and Science* 18 (Fall 1985): 295–310.

Wyschogrod, Edith. "Exemplary Individuals: Towards a Phenomenological Ethics." *Philosophy and Theology* 1 (Fall 1986): 9–31.

————. "Theology in the Wake of the Other." *Journal of American Academy of Religion* 56 (Spring 1988): 115–30.

Wyschogrod, Edith et. als. "On Deconstructing Theology: a Symposium on *Erring: a Postmodern a/theology.*" *Journal of American Academy of Religion* 3 (Fall 1986): 523–57.

Unpublished Material

Diane Louise Prosser. "Body as (Ex)tension or (Re)tension: From 'Serpentine Wanderer' to 'La Mère Qui Jouit' " Paper presented at the Annual meeting of the American Academy of Religion, Kansas City, Missouri, November 1991.

————. "The Body Aesthetics of Wild Being." Paper presented at the Regional Meeting of the Mountain States/Rocky Mountain Meeting of the American Academy of Religion, Colorado Springs, Colorado, May, 1992.

Index